I0458615

Purpose-Driven Entrepreneurship

Reclaim Your Why For Lasting Success

Roger Best

Copyright © 2025 by Roger Best

All rights reserved.

The content contained within this book may not be reproduced, duplicated, or transmitted without direct written permission from the author or the publisher.

Under no circumstances will any blame or legal responsibility be held against the publisher or author for any damages, reparation, or monetary loss due to the information contained within this book, either directly or indirectly.

Legal Notice: This book is copyright protected. It is only for personal use. You cannot amend, distribute, sell, use, quote or paraphrase any part, or the content within this book, without the consent of the author or publisher.

Disclaimer Notice: Please note the information contained within this document is for educational and entertainment purposes only. All effort has been executed to present accurate, up-to-date, reliable, complete information. No warranties of any kind are declared or implied. Readers acknowledge that the author is not engaged in the rendering of legal, financial, medical or professional advice. The content within this book has been derived from various sources. Please consult a licensed professional before attempting any techniques outline in this book.

By reading this document, the reader agrees that under no circumstances is the author responsible for any director or indirect losses incurred as a result of the use of the information contained within this document, including, but not limited to, errors, omissions, or inaccuracies.

Contents

Introduction: The Power of Why   1

1. Every Entrepreneur's Spark   9

2. The Disconnect   17

3. The Benefits of a Strong Why   27

4. Unearthing Your "Why"   37

5. Reflection for Self-Insight   49

6. Journaling Prompts   61

7. Success Begins with Why   73

8. Living Your Why   77

Bonus: A Variation on the Exercise   97

About the Author   105

Also by Roger Best   107

Introduction: The Power of Why

WHEN I FIRST THREW myself into the wild, woolly world of business, I was propelled forward by a heady cocktail of sheer ambition and caffeine. I was, as they say, *hungry*. I wanted success—glorious, shiny success—and all the trimmings that came with it: freedom, flexibility, the ability to knock off early on a Friday and sip something fruity with a tiny umbrella in it.

But here's the thing about entrepreneurial life—it has a sneaky way of pulling the rug out from under you while you're still trying to stand on it. Before long, I was no longer chasing freedom so much as I was sprinting on a treadmill set to "tornado." I'd traded the dream of flexibility for endless task lists that could have wallpapered Buckingham Palace. Days turned into weeks, which turned into years, and there I was, caught in an exhausting, endless loop—working harder than ever, juggling a thousand plates, and still feeling *unfulfilled*. If you've ever spent any quality time with a hamster wheel, you'll know what I mean: spinning, spinning, spinning, but never actually *getting* anywhere.

Of course, I told myself, *"This is just what success looks like, right?"* You put in the hours, the hustle, the late nights—you push harder. Freedom will come, I thought. Any day now. But instead of getting closer to that promised land of life on my terms, I seemed to be drifting further from it, like a rowboat with a broken oar. I was missing dinners, glued to my phone like it held the secrets of the universe, and—here's the kicker—bringing work home with me every night.

Oh, sure, I was "keeping things afloat," but I had the sinking feeling I was also drowning.

And then one night, after yet another of those "just one more task" marathons, I hit a wall. Not literally, though I was tired enough that it wouldn't have surprised me. Something inside me snapped—or maybe, mercifully, clicked. I sat there in the faint glow of my laptop, bleary-eyed and cranky, and I thought: *Why am I doing this? What am I really chasing?* I'd worked so hard for this business, but for what? To wear exhaustion as a badge of honor? To miss my kid's piano recital for the privilege of answering emails at 11 pm?

It was then that I realized something uncomfortably obvious: I'd never truly defined my *Why.* Oh, I had goals, sure—grow the business, hit the next milestone, conquer the world—but I'd never dug deeper than that. I'd never stopped to ask myself what all those achievements were actually *for.*

So I did something radical: I stepped back. I gave myself time to peel back the layers of ambition, ego, and ingrained habits until I got to the truth of it. And what I found was both humbling and liberating. I didn't start this business to "hustle harder" or to be the busiest person at the coffee shop. I started it because I wanted freedom. I wanted to spend real, unhurried time with my family. I wanted to pursue my passions and, maybe, just maybe, help others avoid falling into the same hamster-wheel trap I'd been spinning on.

Once I rediscovered my *Why,* everything began to change. I started making decisions differently. I said "no" to tasks that didn't serve my vision and "yes" to boundaries I'd once considered selfish luxuries—like finishing work at a reasonable hour or, heaven forbid, taking a day off. I delegated like my sanity depended on it (because it did), and slowly but surely, the wheel stopped spinning.

For the first time in ages, I felt clear-headed and—dare I say it—*content.* I wasn't just grinding away anymore; I was building something meaningful. And here's the magic part: that clarity didn't just bring me peace; it helped me guide other frazzled entrepreneurs to find their *own* Why. Because when you know your purpose—when you have that unshakable compass guiding you—it transforms everything. Suddenly, you're not just running a business. You're building a life. A life that means something.

So if you're out there right now, spinning your wheels and wondering if you're the only one—trust me, you're not. I've been there, too. But let me tell you, there's a way out. And it starts with rediscovering your *Why*.

Let's go find it, shall we?

The Power of Why

Ah, yes, let's take a moment, shall we? Close your eyes (metaphorically—this is no time to walk into furniture) and think back to the day you decided to start your business. Maybe you were struck by a brilliant idea that made you feel like one of those inventors from old-timey black-and-white films, the kind who dramatically shouts, *"Eureka!"* as they fling open a door. Or perhaps it was less theatrical—more of a quiet conviction, an itch that wouldn't be scratched, a voice whispering, "There's more out there for you." Whatever it was, you began with that rare and intoxicating mix of hope, optimism, and the deeply held belief that this venture of yours would grant you freedom, fulfillment, and—dare we say it?—a life of balance and flexibility.

And then, well...life happened.

Suddenly, instead of basking in the glow of your entrepreneurial triumph, you found yourself buried under to-do lists that seemed to breed like rabbits. There were long nights where "just one more thing" turned into *five* things, where the only things growing faster than your workload were the bags under your eyes. Stress sidled in like an unwelcome guest who doesn't take hints, and somewhere amidst all the chaos, that spark—that big, beautiful *Why*—started to look suspiciously like an endangered species.

Here's a rather unvarnished truth that's hard to swallow, like cold porridge: not having a clear *Why* is one of the quickest ways for an entrepreneur to end up in the dreaded lands of stuck, overwhelmed, or—heaven help us—ready to throw in the towel. Without a proper purpose tethering us to the ground, we tend to drift aimlessly, like a rogue balloon at a children's birthday party. We get so caught up in the frantic churn of just keeping the business running that we forget what got us started in the first place. And when that happens, even the best-laid plans start to unravel like a cheap sweater.

But here's the good news. A strong, well-defined *Why* is like a compass. A well-worn, trusty old compass you might find in the back pocket of an intrepid explorer. It keeps you headed in the right direction, even when the terrain gets rough. When setbacks inevitably hit—and they will, because life loves a good curveball—it's that *Why* that helps you plant your feet and press forward. It's the thing that nudges you to pull one more late night *when it truly counts* and makes impossible decisions feel just a smidge clearer, because you know what matters most to you.

The story, of course, is not uncommon. Entrepreneurs begin their journeys with fire in their bellies and stars in their eyes, but many overlook this vital piece of the puzzle: a reason so deeply ingrained that no obstacle—not even the maddening frustration of printer jams—can shake it. Without it, they wind up exhausted, grumpy, and prone to muttering questions like, *"Is this all worth it?"* under their breath while staring out of windows dramatically, which is no way to live.

But here's the thing. Reconnecting with your *Why* can turn everything around. It's the difference between going through the motions like some tragic figure on autopilot and actually *building* something meaningful. You don't just need motivation—that runs out, like batteries on an old flashlight. You need a reason so compelling, so intrinsically *you*, that you could stand in a storm and think, *"Nope, I'm still on the right path."*

So that's what we're going to do together in these pages. We're going to unearth your *Why*—dust it off, polish it up, and make it the driving force behind every decision you make, every challenge you face, and every win you celebrate. Because, as any wise old entrepreneur (or at least one with a few bruises and a wry smile) will tell you, the real secret to success lies in staying true to the *Why* that got you started in the first place.

Shall we begin? Splendid. I promise it'll be worth it.

The Hidden Cost of an Undefined Why

It's a curious phenomenon, isn't it? How so many entrepreneurs charge into the world of business with all the enthusiasm of a child let loose in a candy store—eager, optimistic, convinced they're onto something brilliant—without ever stopping to ask themselves the rather fundamental question of *Why*. Now, don't get me wrong. I'm not here to wag my finger. It's much easier to ride the wave of excitement—"This is going to change everything!"—than to sit down with a cup of tea and ponder the deeper existential query of, "What's really driving me to do this?"

But here's where it gets fascinating (and a bit unsettling): According to some very clever people over at Harvard Business School, the absence of a clear purpose isn't just a personal conundrum. Oh no—it's the kind of thing that seeps into the very fabric of a business, like tea spilled on your favorite sofa cushion. Their research shows that a staggering 65% of high-potential startups don't fail because they lacked a great idea or even funding. No, these businesses crumble because their co-founders—those plucky, visionary partners—couldn't align on the big Why. Without that shared purpose, things have a way of unraveling faster than an old jumper snagged on a nail.

I've seen it time and again in my years of coaching entrepreneurs—moments of inspiration followed by the slow, creeping fog of confusion. Entrepreneurs without a clear Why end up adrift, burning out faster than the cheap candles you buy in bulk. Decision-making starts to feel less like a strategy session and more like playing whack-a-mole, trying to knock down one issue after another before another two pop up. That initial enthusiasm—so boundless and electric—begins to fizzle out, sputtering like a lawnmower that hasn't seen maintenance since the Reagan administration.

Soon enough, the grind takes over. Challenges pile up like laundry after a holiday, the to-do list stretches endlessly into the horizon, and the whole endeavor begins to feel suspiciously like that dreaded hamster wheel they set out to escape. You know the one—where you're running at full tilt and still getting nowhere.

And here's the cruel irony: most of these folks started their businesses *precisely* to avoid this very feeling.

But (and this is the part worth highlighting in neon yellow) there's a way out of this cycle. Reconnecting with your Why isn't just a nice idea—it's a game changer. It's like finding a compass in the middle of the woods, suddenly realizing that, no, you're not doomed to wander aimlessly forever. With a clear sense of purpose, obstacles stop feeling like personal affronts and start looking more like milestones. You're no longer spinning your wheels; you're steering toward something meaningful.

And this is where the real magic happens: decisions become easier because they're guided by something deeper than fear or urgency. You act with confidence, handle challenges with a sense of calm, and, perhaps most importantly, rediscover the elusive joy that first sparked your journey.

In the chapters ahead, we'll dig into this together. We'll uncover a purpose that doesn't just give you a reason to get out of bed in the morning but keeps you steady when the storms roll in. Because once you've reconnected with your Why, the day-to-day grind starts to look less like survival and more like progress toward something truly worthwhile.

And trust me, that changes *everything*.

Setting the Tone: The Universal "Why" Challenge

If you're anything like most entrepreneurs—and let's face it, you probably are—you started out with the kind of fiery enthusiasm that could outshine a small supernova. There was this idea, this vision, this brilliantly exciting *thing* that got under your skin and wouldn't let go. It was so electrifying it practically launched you out of bed in the morning, ready to conquer the world with the kind of gusto that would make even the most caffeinated among us envious. You were unstoppable, a force of nature, the entrepreneurial equivalent of a hurricane wrapped in a rainbow.

But then, as these stories often go, life happened. The days piled up like laundry after a holiday, and tasks, emails, meetings, and endless obligations began to stack themselves into a teetering tower of "busyness." That initial spark—the one that burned so brightly it could've powered a small town? Well, it started to dim. Not all at once, of course; these things rarely do. But one day, there you were, staring at a screen or a spreadsheet or maybe the endless abyss of unfinished tasks, wondering, *What happened to me? Where did the excitement go?*

And here's the thing you need to hear: you're not alone. Not even a little bit. Losing sight of your Why—that big, audacious reason you started all this in the first place—is as common as forgetting where you left your keys. It's not a sign that you've failed, or that you're somehow broken, or that it's time to abandon ship and open a llama sanctuary in the Andes (appealing though that sometimes sounds). No, this is just one of those less-than-glamorous detours that comes with the territory.

But here's the good news: it doesn't have to be where your story stalls out. In fact, this moment—frustrating and disorienting as it may feel—can be a pivotal turning point. It's the kind of wake-up call that nudges you to stop, take a step back, and ask yourself the all-important question: *Why did I start this journey in the first place? What was I really chasing?*

Because here's the magic: rediscovering your Why isn't just about reminiscing over where you began. It's about reigniting that spark, that driving force that makes the wild rollercoaster of entrepreneurship not just bearable but downright exhilarating. When you reconnect with your Why, it's like flipping on a light switch in a room you forgot was beautiful. Suddenly, everything feels a little clearer, a little more purposeful, and dare I say it—a little more fun.

That's the thing about purpose: it doesn't just power you through the good days, when everything's coming up roses and your inbox is miraculously empty. It's what gets you through the hard days—the gritty, messy, "why-did-I-ever-think-this-was-a-good-idea" days. Purpose isn't just a motivational poster; it's your compass. It points you back to what matters, even when the road ahead feels like it's paved with potholes and existential dread.

So, if you're feeling a little lost—or like the early excitement has packed its bags and left for greener pastures—don't despair. That's exactly why this book exists. Together, we're going to dig deep, uncover that Why of yours, and polish it until it gleams. We'll make it your guiding star, your north on the compass, your reason to keep going when the going gets tough.

And here's the best part: when your Why is clear, the path ahead doesn't just brighten—it transforms. This isn't the end of your entrepreneurial story. Not by a long shot. This is the beginning of something extraordinary. So, buckle up. The best is yet to come.

Chapter One

Every Entrepreneur's Spark

Every entrepreneur starts with a spark—that thrilling, unmistakable jolt of *Aha!* that propels you headfirst into the adventure of a lifetime. It might've been a wild idea scribbled on the back of a napkin, a vision of freedom so vivid it practically glowed, or perhaps a tiny, stubborn voice in your head saying, *You're meant to build something extraordinary.* Whatever form it took, it was yours. It was exciting. And it was enough to convince you that the late nights, the uncertainty, and the occasional bout of *What on earth am I doing?* were all worth it.

But here's the thing about sparks—they don't exactly come with a lifetime guarantee. The giddy excitement of those early days can fade faster than you'd like to admit once the day-to-day realities of running a business start stacking up. Suddenly, you're knee-deep in spreadsheets, trying to decipher things like tax codes and marketing funnels, and wondering why every email you receive begins with "Just circling back..." Milestones you once dreamed about achieving can begin to feel strangely underwhelming. And before you know it, you're in the trenches, juggling endless tasks, and asking yourself, *Wait, was this what I signed up for?*

That's when true purpose steps in to save the day.

You see, milestones and goals are wonderful—they're like shiny trophies you pick up along the way. But they're not the whole story. They're not what keeps you going when the glow of newness wears off. Your *Why*—that deep, quiet purpose—is the real star of the show. It's not about hitting a target or collecting achievements like a magpie hoarding shiny trinkets. It's the steady, unshakable heartbeat behind everything you do. It's what keeps you moving when the novelty of "being your own boss" turns into managing your own chaos.

For some, that Why is about carving out a life of freedom, where work fits neatly into life instead of devouring it whole. For others, it's about leaving a mark—building something meaningful that proves something to yourself, or perhaps to the world. It's the legacy you want to leave, the difference you want to make, or the dream you refuse to let go of.

Whatever your Why may be, it's deeply personal. It's not something that fits neatly on a motivational poster or in a pithy Instagram caption. It's the thing that feels *right*—that aligns with your values, your priorities, and the person you want to be.

And here's where the magic happens: when you're truly connected to that purpose, everything changes. The grind isn't just a grind anymore; it's part of a much bigger picture. The tough days become steps forward instead of obstacles. Setbacks feel less like failures and more like moments that test and strengthen your resolve. Your Why becomes a compass, pointing you toward decisions that align with your values and keeping you steady when uncertainty clouds your path.

A clear Why doesn't just sustain you—it strengthens you. It becomes the energy you lean on when motivation is running on fumes and the workday stretches endlessly ahead. It helps you make decisions with confidence and without regret. And perhaps most importantly, it keeps you focused on building something that feels *right*—not just impressive, but meaningful.

And here's the best bit: a strong Why isn't a fleeting thing. It grows stronger over time. By Day 1000, it's more powerful than it was on Day 1 because it's been tested. It's guided you through storms and successes alike, proving its worth over and over again.

Defining your Why isn't just some fluffy, feel-good exercise. It's the foundation of everything. It connects you back to the heart of your work, transforming how you approach every challenge, every decision, every triumph. It's what turns the day-to-day slog into a journey filled with clarity, purpose, and—dare I say it—joy.

Because when you know your Why, you're not just building a business; you're creating something bigger. A life. A legacy. A story worth telling.

And trust me, that makes all the difference.

Purpose: Your Anchor in the Storm

In the wonderfully unpredictable world of entrepreneurship—and by *wonderfully*, I mean the sort of unpredictability that makes you question your life choices while nervously eating an entire sleeve of cookies—purpose is your anchor. It's the thing that keeps you tethered when the waves of uncertainty swell up and try to drag you off course.

You can plan all you want. You can have spreadsheets, color-coded calendars, and contingency plans so airtight they'd impress a NASA engineer. But here's the reality: setbacks will come. Plans will unravel. At some point, you'll find yourself staring down a problem so unexpected you'll wonder if the universe is having a laugh at your expense. And in those moments—when doubt whispers in your ear and the temptation to chuck it all and run off to live among the goats in a picturesque village feels *very* real—purpose is what pulls you back.

Your purpose is not just a motivational slogan you scrawl on a sticky note and slap onto your desk. It's the thing that holds you steady when the waves are at their fiercest. It's the voice that calmly, quietly says: *"This is why you're here. This is what matters."*

Think about those moments—those truly heavy moments—when the weight of entrepreneurship presses down hardest. Maybe a plan collapses spectacularly, leaving you staring at the wreckage. Maybe you're working twice as hard and getting half as far. Maybe there's a problem so big and demanding it feels like someone dared it to outdo the last one. That's when your purpose becomes less of a nice-to-have and more of a lifeline. It's what keeps you from throwing up your hands and declaring, "Well, that's it! I'm moving to a cabin and learning how to whittle spoons!"

Purpose reminds you that the hard stuff—the setbacks, the wrong turns, the days where coffee is the only thing holding you together—is not the end of your story. It's just part of the plot.

Even more than that, a clear purpose brings clarity when choices feel murky. You know those decisions that make you pace the room while muttering pros and cons like a mad scientist? Purpose cuts through all that noise. It gives you the confidence to make bold, deliberate moves because you're no longer guessing. You're acting in alignment with your values, your long-term vision, and the bigger picture of what you're building. That's powerful stuff. It's what allows you to stand firm, even when the outcomes aren't guaranteed—because you know *why* you're taking the steps you're taking.

And here's the real magic: your purpose doesn't just shine in the sunny, "everything's going great" moments. Its true strength shows up in the storms. It's what keeps you grounded when the winds howl and the doubts creep in. It's what lets you pause, take a breath, and say, *"I'm staying the course."* Even when external pressures try to nudge you toward the easier, shinier shortcuts, purpose gives you the courage to stay true to your path.

When you build your journey around a strong, deeply personal *Why*, no storm can take you down. Sure, the challenges will come, and sure, they'll test you. But they'll become part of the story—the one you'll look back on someday with a mix of pride, humor, and just enough perspective to say, *"Well, that was a mess, wasn't it?"* And as you move through those challenges, you won't just be surviving them—you'll be growing because of them.

Purpose transforms the whole game. It turns setbacks into stepping stones and gives meaning to every decision, every action, and every long, exhausting day. With purpose as your anchor, you're not just building a business; you're creating something that reflects who you truly are and what matters most to you. And that's a life worth working for, storms and all.

Over the years, I've had the privilege of meeting countless entrepreneurs—bright, driven people with big dreams and a knack for hard work—who, like me, found themselves ensnared in the gears of the relentless daily grind. It's a strange predicament, isn't it? You're working tirelessly, racking up long hours like trophies, yet feeling as though you're somehow running in place, like a character in one of those old cartoons whose legs spin furiously while the background loops endlessly behind them. You're busy—so, so busy—but progress feels maddeningly elusive.

What's fascinating is that while each of these stories is unique—like fingerprints or badly packed suitcases—they all share a common thread: reconnecting with purpose didn't just reignite their passion; it transformed the entire journey.

Take Sarah, for instance. Now, Sarah started her graphic design business with a goal so pure and lovely it could've been written on a tea-stained parchment: she loved creating art and wanted to share something meaningful with the world. And for a while, she *thrived*. She was the very picture of passion-fueled success—coffee cups strewn about, creative sparks flying, the kind of energy that makes you leap out of bed in the morning. But then, as her business grew, something quietly shifted. The joy of creating, the thing that had filled her with life, was slowly nudged aside by deadlines, client demands, and an ever-expanding to-do list that seemed to whisper menacingly, *"More, more, more."*

When we sat down to revisit her *Why*, it was like peeling back the layers of an onion—one that might've made her cry a little. Beneath all the "business growth" chatter, Sarah rediscovered her true purpose: her art wasn't just about income; it was about inspiration. Her *Why* had been buried under obligations, and when she dug it up again, everything changed. She started saying "no"—firm, confident, glorious *no*—to projects that didn't align with her values. She carved out space for personal work that brought her joy. And here's the kicker: her business didn't just *survive* this shift—it *thrived*. Who knew that staying true to yourself could be good for business?

Then there's Mike. Mike is one of those fitness coaches who could probably do a push-up with you sitting on his back while reciting motivational quotes.

He started his business for all the right reasons: he wanted to help people live healthier, happier lives. But somewhere along the line, the numbers hijacked the mission. Revenue targets, client quotas, and social media metrics became the measuring sticks for success. Mike powered through, as one does, believing that hitting those numbers was what "winning" looked like. Until, inevitably, burnout knocked on his door, sat down uninvited, and refused to leave.

When we revisited his *Why*, the realization hit him like a barbell to the chest (in a good way). He wasn't in this for quotas or KPIs; he was in this for *people*. Real people, with real stories, who needed his support to transform their lives. So he refocused—less chasing metrics, more genuine connection. And wouldn't you know it? The success he'd been straining so hard for started coming naturally. Mike was energized again, his clients were happier, and he was doing work that felt deeply meaningful.

And then there's my own story—one that I suspect might sound familiar. I started my businesses with one overarching dream: freedom. The freedom to design a life I loved, to explore the world on a whim, and to seize opportunities without having to check my bank balance or calendar with a sense of dread. But somewhere along the way, that dream got buried. I was working harder than ever, juggling multiple businesses like an overambitious circus performer, and wondering—usually late at night—how the heck I'd ended up here.

The turning point came when I stepped back and asked myself some hard questions. Why had I started all of this in the first place? What was I truly working toward? And what had I lost along the way? Reconnecting with my *Why* reminded me that my goal was never about empire-building or endless expansion—it was about designing a life I could *live*. It was about saying "yes" to adventure, to family, to the things that brought me real joy. Once I had that clarity, I began making decisions differently. I let go of what didn't align with my purpose, made space for what did, and, lo and behold, the freedom I'd been chasing for so long found its way back to me.

The stories of Sarah, Mike, and yes, my own, are proof of something we often forget in the frantic pace of entrepreneurship: purpose is transformative.

When you reconnect with the *Why* that's woven into the fabric of who you are, everything shifts. Suddenly, you're not just grinding away at tasks—you're building a life, a legacy, something meaningful and enduring.

There will always be moments when the path feels unclear. The weight of uncertainty, the tangle of challenges, the nagging sense of *"What am I even doing?"*—it's all part of the journey. But when you return to your *Why*, the one rooted in your deepest values, the path starts to make sense again. That purpose becomes your anchor, your compass, and your fuel. It keeps you grounded through the storms and steady through the highs and lows.

And, perhaps most importantly, it reminds you that this whole journey—every success, every setback, every late night and early morning—isn't just worthwhile. It's meaningful. And that's what makes all the difference.

Exercise: Mapping Your Compass Moments

Objective: To reflect on the pivotal moments in your entrepreneurial journey where your purpose—or lack of it—played a significant role, and to use those insights to reconnect with your Why.

Step 1: Identify Key Moments

Take a few minutes to think about your entrepreneurial journey so far. On a blank sheet of paper or in a journal, create two columns:

- **Moments of Alignment**: List times when you felt deeply connected to your purpose. These could be moments of triumph, satisfaction, or clarity, where everything felt "right." Examples: signing your first meaningful client, solving a problem in a way that felt true to your values, or launching a product that resonated deeply with your vision.

- **Moments of Disconnect**: Now, write down moments when you felt off-course or unmoored. These might be times when you felt overwhelmed, burned out, or unsure why you were pushing so hard. Examples: working long hours without a clear goal, making decisions that didn't align with your values, or feeling like you were spinning your wheels.

Step 2: Reflect on the Patterns

Look at both columns. Ask yourself:

- What was happening during the moments of alignment? Were there specific actions, decisions, or circumstances that kept you connected to your purpose?

- What caused the moments of disconnect? Was it external pressures, unclear goals, or getting caught up in the grind?

Write down any patterns or recurring themes you notice.

Step 3: Reconnect with Your Why

Now, reflect on this:

- During the moments of alignment, what felt most meaningful to you?

- If your Why had a voice during the moments of disconnect, what might it have said?

Jot down a short statement that captures what drives you—your personal Why in its simplest form. Keep it honest and true to who you are.

Step 4: Anchor Your Purpose

To make this exercise actionable, write down one way you can reconnect with your purpose starting today. Maybe it's saying "no" to a task that doesn't align with your values or spending a few minutes journaling about what truly matters to you before tackling your day.

Chapter Two

The Disconnect

In the Glow of Purpose

IN THE EARLY DAYS of starting your own business, purpose is nothing short of a dazzling spotlight, the kind that makes everything around it seem brighter, sharper, and impossibly full of promise. It's that thrilling jolt that launches you out of bed each morning, fueled by the sheer excitement of what lies ahead. The vision is so vivid, so electric, that staying motivated feels as natural as breathing.

But then reality, that wily trickster, saunters in uninvited. It doesn't knock politely or wait to be asked—it just shows up, dumps its bags in your living room, and starts rearranging the furniture. As it turns out, running a business isn't a heroic sprint toward greatness. It's a peculiar mix of sprints, marathons, and, more often than you'd like, obstacle courses designed by someone with a truly wicked sense of humor. Deadlines multiply, responsibilities stack up, and the to-do list develops an unsettling ability to regenerate overnight, like some kind of paperwork hydra.

And slowly—oh so slowly, like watching the sun set on a perfect summer evening—that blazing fire of purpose begins to fade. Not all at once, mind you. That's the sneaky bit. It starts with a thought: *It's just a busy season. I'll push through this, put in a few extra hours, and everything will calm down.* But the busy season doesn't end. It sets up camp, grows roots, and becomes the new normal. Before you know it, you're living in a loop of endless tasks, endless demands, and days that blur together faster than you'd like to admit.

Growth, for all its glittering appeal, tends to arrive with a side order of pressure. More clients, more deadlines, more targets—it's a relentless cycle of *more*. And that's where the hamster wheel trap gets you. You start running, convinced that just a little more effort, a few more sacrifices, and perhaps an industrial-sized pot of coffee will get you to some elusive *there*. Wherever *there* might be.

But "someday," as it turns out, has a frustrating tendency to remain just out of reach. The harder you push, the faster you run, the further away it drifts, like some cruel mirage on the entrepreneurial horizon.

And here's the truly alarming part: it's frighteningly easy to lose sight of your purpose when every day feels like a frantic scramble to keep up. The obligations pile up like an overstuffed backpack, and suddenly, you're checking boxes and chasing goals without really feeling them. Success might come, but it feels oddly hollow, like opening a beautifully wrapped present only to find it empty. The work loses its connection to the Why that made it all so worthwhile in the first place.

But here's the twist: this isn't the end of the story. Not by a long shot.

Recognizing that you've drifted from your purpose is like stumbling across a much-needed trail marker after wandering in circles. Awareness—real, honest awareness—is the first step toward reclaiming that spark, that deeper reason that got you started in the first place.

When you stop—truly stop—and take a moment to breathe, to reflect, to *see* where you are, you give yourself the opportunity to shift. To recalibrate. To remember that this isn't just about grinding through the days. It's about creating meaning. It's about intentionally building a life and a business that reflect your values, your priorities, and the version of yourself you most want to be.

And no, reclaiming your purpose doesn't mean abandoning ambition or tossing your responsibilities into the nearest rubbish bin while you take off on a quest to find yourself. Quite the opposite. It's about rediscovering the joy and the drive that once propelled you and weaving them back into the work you do every day. It's about letting your Why guide you—not just through the hard moments, but toward a future that feels as luminous and full of possibility as the day you began.

Because here's the truth: you don't have to settle for endlessly grinding away in the dark. You can reignite that light. And when you do, something remarkable happens. The work doesn't magically change, but *you* do. Every step, every task, every decision feels intentional, purposeful, and aligned with something that matters deeply to you.

You're no longer running to keep up. You're moving forward—with clarity, with purpose, and with the kind of confidence that comes from knowing you're building a life and a legacy worth chasing.

And that, my friend, is a future truly worth pursuing.

The Slow Fade of Purpose

Losing touch with your purpose doesn't come with a grand announcement or a theatrical crash. No, it's more like a slow leak—subtle, sneaky, and so quiet you barely notice until one day you find yourself running on fumes, wondering how you got there. At first, everything is electric. You're wide-eyed and buzzing with enthusiasm, certain that this idea, this business, this *thing* you're building is going to light up your world.

But then, reality—with all the grace of a clumsy houseguest—starts unpacking its bags. The to-do lists multiply like rabbits, deadlines pile up like laundry, and you begin to wonder if you're the starring act in some cosmic joke. That original excitement? It starts to dim, crowded out by the sheer volume of "stuff" demanding your attention.

And here's the rub: it doesn't happen overnight. At first, you tell yourself, *This is just a busy season. I'll push through, and things will settle.* But the busy season doesn't end—it digs in, sets up shop, and makes itself at home. Before you know it, you're in autopilot mode, trudging through the day with all the vigor of someone folding laundry for the sixth time.

The grind, relentless as it is, begins to take its toll. You wake up tired—not the "hit snooze and rally" kind of tired, but the bone-deep exhaustion that makes you question if coffee has lost its magic. You hit your goals, but they feel oddly hollow, like a gift box with nothing inside. And while you're busy ticking boxes and chasing targets, the thought creeps in: *Why doesn't this feel the way I thought it would?*

Frustration, that sneaky devil, starts bubbling up. Small setbacks turn into monumental irritations, and you find yourself snapping at things that wouldn't have fazed you before. Success—when it finally shows up—feels more like a checkbox than a triumph. Regret sidles in next, whispering about all the time spent chasing motion instead of meaning.

And then there are the relationships—the ones that matter most. Endless hours at your desk, rushed dinners, the glow of your laptop invading what should've been quiet time—it all starts to look like time stolen. Stolen from family moments, from friends who've stopped waiting for you to call, from memories that could've been made. And if you let yourself dwell on it, the guilt can feel as heavy as a stone in your pocket.

This isn't just an emotional toll, mind you. Losing touch with your purpose messes with your head, too. Decision-making turns into a bewildering game of "what if," where every choice feels like a gamble. You say "yes" to things that don't align with your values because "no" feels too risky. Before long, you're scattered, overwhelmed, and drifting further from the vision that once felt so clear.

Even your professional relationships can take a hit. Purpose has a way of bringing people together, of creating shared energy and direction. When that fades, so does the spark in your team, your clients, and your work. Enthusiasm gives way to fatigue, and confidence crumbles into doubt.

But perhaps the greatest cost of all is what it does to *you*. Purpose isn't just about the work—it's about who you are. It's the thread that ties your dreams, values, and ambitions into something meaningful. Without it, you're like a ship without an anchor, drifting further and further from where you want to be.

And yet—here's the hopeful twist—realizing this disconnection isn't a failure. It's a gift. Awareness is the first step to change. Recognizing that you've lost touch with your Why is like finding a trail marker in a dense forest. It's your chance to pause, reassess, and choose a better path.

When you reconnect with your purpose, the transformation is remarkable. Work stops feeling like an endless grind and starts to mean something again. Decisions feel deliberate, guided by clarity instead of panic. And that spark—the one you thought had gone out—flares back to life, brighter and steadier than before.

Rediscovering your Why doesn't just change your business; it changes *you*. It brings balance to your days, fulfillment to your efforts, and joy back to the journey.

And here's the best bit: it's never too late. Never too late to reignite that spark, to reclaim the meaning, excitement, and freedom that set you on this path in the first place. So, take a deep breath. The spark is still there, waiting for you to find it.

And when you do, everything changes.

The Cycle of Hustle: A Reflection from "From Hamster Wheel to Hammock"

In *From Hamster Wheel to Hammock*, we tackled a cycle that feels all too familiar to most entrepreneurs—a loop so relentless it could have been dreamed up by Sisyphus himself. It's the grind, the hustle, the endless stream of tasks that always seem to multiply like gremlins when your back is turned. Days blur into weeks, and before you know it, you're living the entrepreneurial version of *Groundhog Day*, running harder and faster but never quite escaping the nagging sense of being perpetually "on."

We're told the hustle is noble—that it's the price of admission to the golden land of freedom, success, and balance. "If I just push a little harder," we whisper to ourselves during yet another late night, "if I work a bit longer, skip that dinner, or sacrifice just a little more sleep—then, surely, the rewards will come." But here's the catch: for most of us, that relentless cycle doesn't bring us closer to the life we envisioned. Instead, it pulls us further away, dragging us from the very dreams that set us on this path in the first place.

It's like spending years on a treadmill that speeds up whenever we dare to reach for the "stop" button. You're left panting, dizzy, and utterly bewildered, wondering how so much effort could leave you feeling so far from freedom. And the worst part? You don't even notice it happening until you're knee-deep in exhaustion, disconnection, and the faint memory of why you started this journey at all.

In *From Hamster Wheel to Hammock*, I shared how easy it is to fall into the trap of believing success demands sacrifice—the kind of sacrifice that devours your time, health, relationships, and, perhaps most tragically, your passions. We tell ourselves, "It's fine, it's temporary. Once I've made it, I'll slow down. I'll relax. I'll live the life I've been putting off." But without a clear purpose as our compass—without that solid, steady *Why* to guide us—"someday" becomes a mirage. No matter how fast or far we run, it remains tantalizingly out of reach.

The lesson, while simple, is one of the hardest truths to live by: staying connected to your purpose isn't a luxury; it's a lifeline. It's what transforms the grind from an endless race into a deliberate journey. Purpose doesn't just nudge us forward; it anchors us, giving weight and meaning to our decisions. It reminds us that success isn't just about checking boxes—it's about creating a life that reflects our values, one where professional success and personal fulfillment can coexist.

In *From Hamster Wheel to Hammock*, we explored what often feels like a radical idea: escaping the hamster wheel doesn't mean working harder; it means working smarter. It means stepping off the treadmill and deciding that your life will no longer be ruled by the endless churn of busyness. It means reconnecting with the deeper purpose that drives you and using that purpose to shape a life that's not only productive but also joyful.

Here's the magic: when you remember those lessons and apply them—when you let your *Why* steer the ship—everything changes. The grind loses its grip. Decisions become clearer. The noise of constant demands fades, replaced by a sense of calm and clarity. You stop surviving and start thriving—not in a superficial, "look how busy I am" way, but in a deeply fulfilling, sustainable way that feels uniquely yours.

That's the vision we're chasing—not a finish line you're too weary to cross, but a life you're fully present for. A life where success isn't measured by how much you've sacrificed but by how well you've lived. And let me tell you, that's a life worth running toward—one intentional, joyful step at a time.

Reclaiming Focus

Realizing you've drifted from your original purpose can be one of those gut-punch moments—the kind that sneaks up on you, like finding yourself halfway through a bag of chips without recalling how it started. It's unsettling, to be sure. One day, you're charging forward, full of ambition and optimism, and the next, you're staring down the chaos of your daily grind thinking, "Hold on—how did I get here?"

But as disorienting as that moment might feel, it's also a gift. Truly. Like realizing mid-hike that you've been following the wrong trail—it's frustrating, sure, but now you know, and you can course-correct. That awareness is the spark, the beginning of something better. It's the nudge you need to pause, take stock, and declare, "This isn't what I signed up for. I want more than this."

Let's get one thing straight: recognizing this drift isn't failure. It's clarity. It's that crucial turning point where you reclaim control, yank the wheel from autopilot, and start steering intentionally. You stop running just to keep up and start choosing your direction with purpose. It's the moment you look back at where you've been, where you want to go, and—perhaps most importantly—what truly matters to you.

Reconnecting with your purpose is like flipping a switch. Choices no longer feel like a frantic game of whack-a-mole; they feel deliberate, meaningful. Each decision you make becomes a step toward a life and business that align with who you are, not just what's expected of you. This isn't about abandoning ambition—far from it. Ambition, when tied to purpose, becomes a force to be reckoned with. It's about making your goals meaningful again, so that success doesn't feel like some hollow trophy but resonates deep in your soul.

At its heart, reclaiming focus is about taking back control—control of your time, your energy, and, most importantly, the deeper reasons you show up every day. It's an invitation to quiet the noise: the distractions, the busyness, the endless cycle of "more" that doesn't serve you. It's a chance to reconnect with the heart of what drives you. And when you do, something remarkable happens. Clarity returns. Energy resurfaces. That sense of purpose you thought was long gone? It's back, ready to guide you forward.

This isn't just a gentle nudge or minor tweak. It's a transformation. It's about rediscovering the joy, the spark, the *Why* that lit your path in the beginning. It's about reconnecting with the reason you were willing to sacrifice, to persevere, to push through the tough times. Because when you know your *Why*, even the hard days make sense. They become stepping stones in a journey worth taking, not just another mile in a meaningless marathon.

And here's the liberating truth: you can choose a different path at any time. Always. You can hit pause, reflect, and realign with what feels true to you. That single choice—to stop, to remember what matters, and to act on it—can change everything.

So take a breath. Look around. And know this: the spark that got you started isn't gone. It's still there, waiting for you to rediscover it. All it takes is one choice to move closer to the life and business you truly want. And when you make that choice? Oh, the difference it will make.

Exercise: The Purpose Alignment Check-In

Take some time—15 to 20 minutes in a quiet space—to reflect on the following questions. Write your thoughts down honestly and without judgment. This exercise isn't about perfection; it's about uncovering where you are and where you want to be.

Step 1: Recognize the Drift

1. Think back to when you started your business. What excited you most about it? What was the dream that drove you forward?

2. Compare that vision to your current reality. What feels different? Where do you notice a gap between what you wanted and what you have now?

3. Identify three specific ways you feel disconnected from the purpose that inspired you in the beginning.

Step 2: Uncover the Impact

1. How has this drift affected your work? For example, do you feel less motivated, overwhelmed, or stuck in a grind that doesn't feel fulfilling?

2. How has it impacted your personal life? Are there relationships, passions, or self-care routines that have taken a backseat?

3. What emotions come up when you think about the disconnect? Frustration, regret, guilt—or perhaps a sense of opportunity?

Step 3: Reconnect with Your Purpose

1. Rewrite your original "Why." What is the deeper purpose that truly drives you? (If you're unsure, think about what brings you joy, what you value most, and the legacy you want to create.)

2. What's one small but meaningful action you can take this week to realign with your purpose? It could be saying no to something that doesn't serve you, carving out time for something that reignites your passion, or revisiting a goal that excites you.

Step 4: Commit to Realignment

1. Write down three habits or practices you can incorporate into your routine to stay connected to your purpose. This might include journaling, revisiting your "Why" regularly, or creating space for reflection.

2. Set a reminder to revisit this exercise in a month. Use it as a checkpoint to see how far you've come and where you can make further adjustments.

Reflection

Purpose isn't a "set it and forget it" thing. It evolves as we grow, as our businesses change, and as life throws its curveballs. This exercise is your chance to pause, recalibrate, and ensure that your work and life reflect the values that matter most to you. Remember, it's never too late to realign with what truly drives you—and the journey to reclaiming that purpose starts with this first step.

Chapter Three

The Benefits of a Strong Why

Making Purposeful Decisions

WHEN YOU'RE ANCHORED IN a clear sense of purpose, decision-making—once a hair-pulling tug-of-war of overthinking and endless "what-ifs"—becomes something far simpler and more, dare I say, *elegant*. Your *Why* steps in like an old, trusted friend, calmly filtering out the noise and illuminating what truly matters. Gone are the days of sprawling pros-and-cons lists scrawled in fits of indecision. Instead, your purpose becomes a sort of internal compass, nudging you gently toward choices that align with who you are and where you want to go.

Now, I'm not saying you'll suddenly find yourself skipping through fields of daisies, blissfully immune to tough calls. Entrepreneurs face a maze of decisions on a daily basis—whether to take on that new client, launch a product, grow the team, or maybe just find time to drink a proper cup of coffee. But here's the magic: when you're rooted in your *Why*, those choices stop feeling like a relentless reaction to life's curveballs and start feeling like deliberate, intentional steps toward the vision you've created.

Take, for instance, the temptation of a shiny, lucrative partnership that looks dazzling on paper but doesn't align with your values. Without a clear sense of purpose, it's easy to say "yes" out of fear—fear of missing out, fear of turning down growth, fear that opportunity won't come knocking twice. But when your *Why* is clear, the decision practically makes itself. You can see, with startling clarity, that saying "yes" to something that doesn't fit means saying "no" to what truly matters. It's a powerful reminder that short-term gains aren't worth the long-term misalignment of your vision.

That's the beauty of being purpose-driven: even tough calls feel *right*. They may still sting a little—turning down an opportunity often does—but you won't lose sleep over them. You'll know, deep down, that you're prioritizing the long game, and that's where the real magic happens.

This clarity doesn't just shape the "big" decisions either—it trickles into the little things, too. Delegating a task, choosing which projects to pursue, even deciding how to spend a free hour—every choice becomes infused with meaning. You're no longer just ticking boxes or hitting arbitrary milestones for the sake of it. Instead, you're building something with intention. Something that reflects your values and leaves an impact you're proud of.

And here's the thing: alignment feels *good*. Really good. When your decisions flow naturally from your purpose, there's this sense of quiet fulfillment that's hard to replicate. You stop second-guessing yourself or looking over your shoulder, wondering if you made the "right" choice. Instead, you move forward with confidence, knowing that every "yes" and every "no" is helping you create a life and business that truly matter to *you*.

A strong *Why* doesn't just make decisions easier; it makes them *meaningful*. It's your compass, steady and reliable, steering you through the complexities of entrepreneurship with focus and clarity. It's the thing that reminds you that every choice—no matter how small—is an opportunity to align your work with your values, to craft something that reflects not just what you do, but *who you are*.

And as you continue making these purpose-driven choices, you'll find you're not just running a business. You're building a legacy—one thoughtful decision at a time—that reflects the very best of who you are and the life you set out to create. And that, my friend, is where the magic really lies.

Experiencing Personal Fulfillment

There's something profoundly satisfying—*transformative*, even—about being in sync with a purpose that truly matters to you. It's like flipping a switch on the work you do every day. Suddenly, it's not just a conveyor belt of tasks or an endless parade of obligations; it becomes something *meaningful*. Each step, no matter how seemingly small, feels like a deliberate move toward a vision that lights you up inside.

When you reconnect with your purpose, everything gets a little richer, a little deeper. Fulfillment stops being that elusive treasure you'll stumble upon *someday*, at some imaginary finish line, and instead becomes something you can find right here, today, in the middle of the journey.

Even the routine moments take on a new hue when you're clear on your *Why*. The late nights, once fueled by caffeine and quiet desperation, suddenly feel less like sacrifices and more like investments in something you genuinely believe in. The small wins—those tiny victories that used to barely register—start to feel like joyful little reminders that you're moving in the right direction. You're not just grinding through another day; you're building something that matters, guided by your values and your vision.

And here's the thing: this sense of fulfillment isn't fleeting. It's not the hollow, sugar-rush satisfaction you get from checking a box or meeting a deadline just to say you did. It's steady. Grounding. The kind of satisfaction that sinks into your bones and makes even the hard days feel worthwhile. It brings a quiet resilience to your work, helping you face the inevitable ups and downs of entrepreneurship with more grace and far less grumbling.

Because when purpose is your anchor, you're no longer chasing some distant "someday" to finally feel successful or accomplished. You realize that fulfillment doesn't live in some far-off future. It's right here, in the choices you make every day, the people you connect with, and the life you're intentionally shaping.

Purpose also has this sneaky way of reframing how you see the journey itself. Instead of racing toward a finish line, you begin to appreciate the process—*really* appreciate it. The highs become worth celebrating, and the lows, rather than feeling like failures, become essential plot points in a larger, more meaningful story. *Your* story.

When you're anchored in your deeper *Why*, each day holds its own kind of potential. It's no longer just about hitting goals or ticking boxes—it's about building a life that reflects who you truly are and what you value most. You start to find joy in the process, knowing that what you're creating is authentic, intentional, and deeply meaningful.

And that, I think, is the real magic of it all. Reconnecting with purpose doesn't just change your business; it changes how you *feel* about the work itself. It reminds you that you're not floundering, you're not just surviving—you're *exactly* where you're supposed to be, building a life that's uniquely yours. And in a world where so many people are just going through the motions, that's no small thing.

So take a moment. Look around. You're not just moving forward; you're creating something that matters, day by day, choice by choice. And honestly, what could be more powerful than that?

Sustaining Through Challenges

Every entrepreneur hits those moments—the ones that test your resolve and leave you staring at the ceiling at 2 a.m., asking yourself life's greatest hits: *Why did I start this? Is it worth it? And where is all this coffee actually going?* It's the setbacks, the tough decisions, the maddening uncertainty that seem tailor-made to shake your confidence and make you second-guess everything.

But here's the thing about purpose: it doesn't wave a magic wand and make those obstacles vanish. Instead, it gives you something far more valuable—*the strength to face them*. When you're grounded in a strong, deeply personal sense of *Why*, those struggles shift. They're no longer just obstacles; they're stepping stones—unpleasant, ankle-twisting stepping stones, maybe, but stepping stones nonetheless—pushing you forward toward something that truly matters.

A clear purpose is like that old, sturdy lighthouse on a stormy night. It's steady, unwavering, and always there, quietly reminding you: *This is why you're here. This is why it matters.* And when doubt sneaks in, as it inevitably does, that connection to your *Why* brings you back to the bigger picture. You start to see the struggle not as a sign to pack it in, but as a test—one that challenges your commitment, deepens your resilience, and, more often than not, leaves you stronger for having faced it.

That's not to say setbacks magically become enjoyable (let's not kid ourselves). They still sting. They still make you mutter colorful words under your breath. But when you're rooted in purpose, they feel different. Instead of overwhelming roadblocks, they become opportunities to pause, reflect, and—if necessary—pivot. They're a chance to grow, to get creative, and to reaffirm what got you on this path in the first place. And here's the reward: every time you overcome one, you're reminded of your own resilience and the value of the vision you're building.

Think about those moments when the climb feels steep, the hours drag on, and the results lag stubbornly behind your effort. Without purpose, those days can feel like quicksand—sapping your energy and leaving you wondering if you're sinking for good. But when you're connected to a purpose bigger than the moment, the equation changes. The challenges, while still tough, feel *worthwhile*. They're no longer just struggles to endure; they're chapters in a story that's uniquely yours—a story of grit, growth, and unshakable belief in what you're creating.

Now, let's be clear: purpose doesn't mean blind optimism or adopting a "just push harder" mantra while ignoring reality. It's not about stubbornly plowing through challenges at the cost of your health, sanity, or relationships. Purpose is smarter than that. It's about knowing that even when the road gets rough—when the winds blow and the wheels wobble—you're on that road for a reason. It's about seeing the struggle not as a failure, but as a refining process, one that sharpens your vision and makes the eventual victories that much sweeter.

In the end, it's the resilience fueled by purpose that carries you through those low points. It's what gets you up on the mornings when motivation feels like it's gone on vacation without you. It's what reminds you that your work—this thing you're pouring yourself into—*matters*. Not just to the world, but to *you*.

With purpose as your foundation, every challenge becomes another step forward, every setback an opportunity to grow, and every hard-won victory a testament to the strength, clarity, and resolve that only a deeply rooted *Why* can provide.

So, when the path feels uncertain, when the doubts start doing their little dance, hold onto that purpose like the lifeline it is. Because, in the end, it's the very thing that will keep you moving—and remind you why every ounce of effort is worth it.

Creativity Rooted in Purpose

There's something almost magical that happens when an entrepreneur reconnects with their purpose—like watching a fog lift and suddenly seeing the landscape that's been there all along. When you're grounded in your *Why*, your work stops being a mechanical series of tasks to plow through and instead becomes a living, breathing expression of who you are and what you stand for. The grind softens. The frustrations ease. Challenges that once felt like brick walls turn into open doors marked *"Opportunity Here—Please Enter."*

It's a remarkable shift. Decisions that used to feel like boxes to check—"Do we need this? Should I do that?"—take on meaning because they're tied to something bigger. They're not just decisions; they're *choices*, infused with intention and aligned with the vision that sets your soul on fire. The daily operations, which can so easily bog you down, start to feel like fertile ground for creativity rather than quicksand for your energy. Purpose asks you to pause and consider: *What can I bring to this that no one else can?* And once you ask yourself that, everything changes.

Because here's the thing about purpose—it unlocks curiosity and courage. It nudges you gently (and sometimes not-so-gently) to think beyond the "right" way to do something, beyond the conventional wisdom that tells you how it's always been done. You stop looking for templates to copy or trends to chase and start tapping into something far more valuable: your own unique vision. Suddenly, "business as usual" feels too small, too ordinary, because now you're creating solutions, products, and experiences that aren't just *successful*. They're *you*.

This is where creativity really comes alive. It's not creativity for its own sake—endlessly pushing boundaries because that's what businesses are told to do. No, it's creativity that's anchored in your values and your vision. It's the kind of creativity that sets your business apart in ways that actually *matter*. Whether you're designing products, shaping team culture, or having a simple conversation with a customer, everything becomes an authentic expression of your purpose. It's not just about standing out; it's about standing true.

And here's where the magic really sparkles: people *notice*. Customers notice. Your team notices. Even collaborators, competitors, and passersby with half an eye on what you're doing will notice. When your work comes from a place of purpose and authenticity, it resonates. It feels alive. It feels real. People don't just see a business that's ticking boxes—they see a business that cares, that means something. And in a world drowning in noise and sameness, that kind of authenticity is memorable.

Think about it: when you're connected to your *Why*, you're not just pushing through another meeting or solving yet another problem. You're creating something *meaningful*—something that reflects who you are and the change you want to make in the world. That energy infuses every part of your work, from brainstorming big ideas to answering emails. It's not just productive; it's *energizing*. It doesn't just help you navigate challenges; it makes the challenges worthwhile because you know they're part of something much bigger.

This alignment is where the real magic happens. Your purpose becomes the spark that ignites your best ideas, the foundation that gives you confidence when things get messy, and the compass that keeps you pointed in the right direction.

It's what helps you build a business that isn't just innovative, but also unmistakably *yours*.

So, when you find yourself stuck, wondering where the creativity's gone or why the grind feels heavier than it should, take a moment. Reconnect with your *Why*. It's not just motivational fluff—it's fuel. It's the thing that transforms your work from a list of tasks into a legacy you can be proud of. And once you find that spark again, well, let's just say that *everything* gets a little brighter.

Exercise: Purpose in Action Journal

The benefits of a strong *Why* don't just exist in theory—they show up in the choices you make, the fulfillment you feel, and the way you approach challenges and opportunities. Use this journal exercise to reflect on how your *Why* has guided you and explore ways to deepen its impact in your life and work.

Step 1: Reflect on Past Decisions

Think about a recent decision you made—big or small. Ask yourself:

1. How did your *Why* influence that choice?

2. Did the decision align with your values and deeper purpose? Why or why not?

3. If the decision didn't align with your *Why*, what might you have done differently?

Step 2: Fulfillment Inventory

1. List three moments in your entrepreneurial journey when you felt truly fulfilled. What made those moments meaningful?

2. How did those moments connect to your *Why*?

3. Reflect on whether your current daily work includes elements that bring you this sense of fulfillment. If not, what can you adjust to bring more of that into your routine?

Step 3: Challenges Reframed

1. Recall a challenge you've faced recently. What made it difficult, and how did you handle it?

2. Reflect on how your *Why* could have supported you during that time. Did it provide resilience or clarity? If not, why?

3. Identify one way to approach future challenges with your *Why* at the forefront.

Step 4: Creativity and Purpose

1. Think of a problem you're currently facing in your business. Write it down.

2. Imagine approaching this issue with your *Why* as your compass. How might that influence the way you solve it?

3. Brainstorm at least three creative solutions inspired by your purpose.

Step 5: Looking Ahead

1. Write down one specific action you'll take this week to strengthen the connection between your *Why* and your decisions, fulfillment, resilience, or creativity.

2. Set a reminder to revisit this journal entry in a month and reflect on the progress you've made.

Reflection

This exercise is designed to help you see the tangible ways your *Why* can shape your decisions, actions, and mindset. By intentionally reflecting on its impact, you'll strengthen your connection to your purpose and begin to experience the benefits of a strong *Why* in every aspect of your journey. Remember, your *Why* is your greatest tool—use it often, and let it guide you toward a life and business that truly reflect who you are.

Chapter Four

Unearthing Your "Why"

As WE DIVE INTO Chapter 4, I hope you're ready to roll up your sleeves—because this chapter isn't for passive readers or casual skimmers. Oh no. This is about doing the work—*the real work*—to uncover your true *Why*. Think of it as less of a chapter and more of a guided excavation. We're about to dig beneath the surface, past all the generic answers and shiny ambitions, and get to the core of what truly drives you.

Now, I know what you're thinking: *"Surely I already know my purpose. I've got goals, a vision board, and a motivational quote saved on my phone."* But this isn't about a quick answer or crafting a slogan that sounds good on a T-shirt. This is about peeling back the layers, one by one, until you hit the bedrock—the deeply personal purpose that fuels you, that gets you out of bed even on the mornings when the to-do list feels longer than the Great Wall of China.

Through a series of thought-provoking questions and reflections, we'll explore the motivations running beneath the surface. This isn't about what sounds impressive or what other people expect of you. This is about *you*: the values that light you up, the dreams that tug at your heart, and the driving force behind why you're on this journey in the first place.

And here's the thing: there's no rush. Uncovering your *Why* isn't a sprint—it's more like patiently untangling a knotted necklace. Take your time. Be honest with yourself. If you let it, this process will reveal something bigger than your daily grind or your next milestone. It will connect you to a purpose that not only inspires you but sustains you through the inevitable ups, downs, and sideways loops of entrepreneurship.

By the time you reach the end of this chapter, you'll have more than just a clearer understanding of what motivates you—you'll have a compass. A guiding star. A *Why* so deeply rooted that it becomes the reason you push through the challenges and the reward that makes it all worth it.

So take a deep breath, grab a notebook (and maybe a fresh cup of coffee), and let's get to work. You're about to uncover something extraordinary—the purpose that's been there all along, waiting for you to find it.

Guided Exercise: Uncovering Your "Why" with the Five Whys Technique

This exercise is all about getting to the *real* heart of things—the core motivation that drives you. Not the polished, surface-level answer you might toss out at a networking event, but the deeper *Why* that makes everything—yes, even the hard stuff—worthwhile.

The way we're going to do this is simple but powerful: we're going to keep asking "Why?" over and over (and then once or twice more for good measure). It sounds deceptively straightforward, but here's the trick—it forces you to dig. To move past the obvious answers and uncover the purpose hiding beneath the surface.

Now, grab a journal or notebook—something you can scribble in without fear of judgment—and find a quiet corner where you can think. Take a deep breath. There's no rush here. This isn't about finding the *perfect* answer; it's about uncovering the *true* one.

And because we need a starting point, we'll kick things off with a simple first question. You might peek ahead and notice there are Six Whys coming your way, but don't panic—I'm not counting the first one. The first question is just the doorway; the good stuff happens when we keep stepping further inside.

So let's begin:

Step 1: Starting Question – Why Did I Start My Business?

Let's keep it simple to begin with. Imagine you're chatting with a friend over coffee, and they ask you, "So, why did you start your business?" What's the first thing that comes to mind? No overthinking, no second-guessing—just the honest, straightforward answer that naturally bubbles up.

Maybe it's:

- "I wanted to be my own boss."

- "I wanted to have financial freedom."

- "I saw a problem I could solve and decided to go for it."

- "I wanted to build something meaningful."

Whatever it is, *write it down*. This isn't the time for polished, profound reflections—this is the spark, the thing that got you out of the gate. It might feel basic, practical, or even obvious, and that's perfectly fine.

Why is this first answer important? Because every journey starts somewhere. By honoring the reason that first drew you in, however simple it might seem, you're setting the stage to dive deeper. Think of this as the surface layer we're about to peel back.

Example: I wanted to be my own boss.

Go ahead—write yours. Trust that this is exactly where you need to start.

Step 2: First "Why?" – Why Is [Your Step 1 Answer} Important to Me?

Now let's take that answer from Step 1—whether it's "I wanted to be my own boss," "I wanted financial freedom," or "I wanted to make a difference"—and ask the next question: **Why is that important to me?**

This is where we start peeling back the layers. Don't settle for the first thought that pops into your head—take a moment and really consider it. What is it about *being your own boss*, or *having financial freedom*, or *making a difference* that feels significant to *you personally*?

For example, let's say your Step 1 answer was "I wanted to be my own boss." Why does that matter? Maybe it's because being your own boss gives you the freedom to make decisions without having to run them by someone else. Maybe it's the independence of creating your own schedule—working when you're at your best instead of being confined to a rigid 9-to-5. Or maybe it's about having control over the projects you choose, the people you work with, and the path you take.

The goal here is to start uncovering the deeper value behind your initial answer. This second layer might point to things like freedom, autonomy, creativity, or even a desire for control—all of which tell you something meaningful about what truly matters to you.

Write your answer down clearly. Let it be honest, even if it surprises you. This step gives depth to that initial spark of motivation and brings you closer to understanding the core values shaping your journey.

Example:

- *Step 1:* I wanted to be my own boss.

- *Step 2:* Being my own boss means I have control over my time and decisions.

See how that starts to deepen things? In this case, the value behind "being my own boss" is *freedom*—freedom to choose, to prioritize, to steer the ship on your terms. That's where the good stuff lives.

Now it's your turn. Write it down, and let's keep digging—you're getting closer to uncovering the purpose that fuels you.

Step 3: Second "Why?" – Why Do I Want Control Over My Time and Decisions?

Now let's take that next step. You've uncovered that having control over your time and decisions matters to you—*but why?* What does that control actually *mean* in your life? What does it enable? How does it shape your experiences, your relationships, and your sense of fulfillment?

Here's where we go deeper. This isn't just about flexibility or freedom for freedom's sake—it's about *what that freedom gives you.* For many, control over time means being able to prioritize what matters most, like spending quality time with family, nurturing creative passions, taking care of their health, or simply creating space for peace of mind. For others, it might be about avoiding the regret of missed moments, reclaiming their energy, or living in a way that feels intentional and aligned.

Take a minute to reflect:

- Why does it matter to *you* that you get to decide where your time and energy go?

- What would you be missing out on if you didn't have that control?

- How does this autonomy bring fulfillment or joy to your life?

Write down your answer, and let yourself dig into both the practical benefits and the emotional rewards. This is where we start to see your values take shape.

Example:

- *Step 1:* I wanted to be my own boss.

- *Step 2:* Being my own boss means I have control over my time and decisions.

- *Step 3:* Control over my time allows me to create a life that prioritizes my family and personal passions.

Here, the deeper motivation begins to emerge. It's not just about setting your own hours or being the one calling the shots—it's about designing a life that aligns with what matters most to you. It's about *presence* with your family, space for what brings you joy, and the freedom to live intentionally, not reactively.

This step brings you closer to understanding the purpose driving your work. You're uncovering the "why behind the why"—the deeply personal motivations that give meaning to your journey and ensure that the business you're building reflects the life you truly want.

Go ahead—write it down. You're starting to see the bigger picture come into focus.

Step 4: Third "Why?" — Why Do I Want a Life That Prioritizes My Family and Passions?

Now we're really getting to the good stuff. By this point, you've uncovered that you want control over your time to build a life that prioritizes your family and personal passions. But let's go one step deeper: *Why does this specific goal matter so much to you?*

What is it about your family and passions that brings you a sense of fulfillment? Is it the joy of being truly present with loved ones, creating moments and memories you'll carry for a lifetime? Or is it about the freedom to express yourself, to do what makes you feel alive and aligned with your truest self? Perhaps it's about avoiding the regret of missing out on what truly matters, ensuring that your time and energy go toward the things that make life feel rich, rewarding, and complete.

Think about the impact:

- How does prioritizing family and passions make your life *better*?

- What would life feel like without those connections and moments?

- How does this align with your values, your beliefs, or even the person you strive to be?

Write this answer down with honesty and care. The deeper you go, the clearer the emotional rewards of your journey become.

Example:

- *Step 1:* I wanted to be my own boss.

- *Step 2:* Being my own boss means I have control over my time and decisions.

- *Step 3:* Control over my time allows me to create a life that prioritizes my family and personal passions.

- *Step 4:* Prioritizing my family and passions gives me a sense of fulfillment and balance.

Here, the layers are starting to converge. It's no longer about the work alone—it's about *how* the work supports what matters most to you. It's about building a life that feels whole and intentional, one where you're not just existing or checking boxes, but truly living.

This answer starts to shine a light on your core values: connection, balance, joy, and being true to who you are. These are the anchors of your *Why*, the fuel that keeps you going when the challenges come.

Take a moment to sit with what you've written. You're getting closer to the heart of your purpose—one that's not just about business success, but about living a life that feels *rich, connected,* and authentically yours.

Step 5: Fourth "Why?" – Why Is Fulfillment and Balance Important to Me?

This is where we uncover the deepest layers of what drives you—your core values, your aspirations, and the essence of who you are (or who you're striving to become). Fulfillment and balance are big, beautiful ideas, but let's pause and ask: *Why do they matter to me personally?*

Take a moment to reflect.

- What does fulfillment mean to you? Is it about peace, contentment, or the ability to live without regret?

- Why does balance resonate so deeply? Does it help you feel grounded, authentic, and connected to the people and passions that matter most?

- How does living with fulfillment and balance allow you to feel like you're being true to yourself?

Maybe you've spent years on the hamster wheel, feeling like life was slipping by as you chased goals that didn't truly reflect who you are. Maybe you've experienced what it's like to feel *unbalanced*, overwhelmed, and disconnected, and now you're determined to create something better. Or perhaps it's simpler: balance and fulfillment just *feel right*, like life falling into harmony instead of chaos.

Ask yourself this, too: *What would it mean for you to live a life centered around fulfillment and balance?* Imagine looking back on your journey, knowing you honored those values. How would it feel?

Write it down. Let this answer capture why these qualities resonate so deeply and how they help you live a life that feels meaningful, aligned, and true to who you are.

Example:

- *Step 1:* I wanted to be my own boss.

- *Step 2:* Being my own boss means I have control over my time and decisions.

- *Step 3:* Control over my time allows me to create a life that prioritizes my family and personal passions.

- *Step 4:* Prioritizing my family and passions gives me a sense of fulfillment and balance.

- *Step 5:* Fulfillment and balance help me feel that I'm living a life that's true to myself and meaningful.

Here's where the heart of your purpose really begins to shine. Fulfillment and balance aren't just ideas—they're part of the foundation of a life that feels *right* for you. They ensure that the path you're walking is one you can look back on with pride, peace, and satisfaction.

This answer brings your purpose into focus: it's about living authentically, with meaning and intention. You're building not just a business but a life—a life that reflects the best of who you are and what you value most.

Sit with this answer for a moment. Let it sink in. You're uncovering the *why behind the why behind the why*—and this clarity is powerful. It's the foundation of a purpose that can guide you through the highs, lows, and everything in between. You're almost there.

Step 6: Fifth "Why?" – Why Is Living a Life That's True to Myself Meaningful to Me?

Here we are—the deepest layer, the place where you uncover the core of what truly drives you. At this stage, you've explored fulfillment, balance, authenticity, and alignment with what matters most. Now it's time to ask: *Why does living a life that's true to myself hold such profound meaning?*

This is where you connect with your essence—your values, your beliefs, the person you are at your core, and the legacy you want to leave behind.

- What does it mean to live in alignment with your true self? Is it about wholeness—knowing that your actions, values, and intentions are woven seamlessly together into a life that feels right?

- Does it reflect the freedom to look back one day, free of regret, confident that every step you took honored your deepest beliefs?

- Or is it about something bigger—leaving a lasting impact? Maybe you want to inspire others—your family, your friends, your team, or your community—to live authentically themselves, setting an example of integrity, purpose, and courage.

Write your answer down with the same honesty and reflection you've brought to this journey so far. This is the essence of *you*—the values that define your purpose and the impact you wish to make on the world.

Example:
- *Step 1:* I wanted to be my own boss.

- *Step 2:* Being my own boss means I have control over my time and decisions.

- *Step 3:* Control over my time allows me to create a life that prioritizes my family and personal passions.

- *Step 4:* Prioritizing my family and passions gives me a sense of fulfillment and balance.

- *Step 5:* Fulfillment and balance help me feel that I'm living a life that's true to myself and meaningful.

- *Step 6:* Living a life true to myself allows me to leave a legacy and make a positive impact on my family and community.

At this final layer, you've uncovered the purpose that fuels you—not just in your business, but in every corner of your life. Living a life that's true to yourself isn't just about feeling fulfilled; it's about creating a legacy of authenticity, integrity, and impact that endures. It's about making choices that align with who you are, leaving behind something meaningful for those around you.

This clarity becomes more than just motivation—it becomes a guiding force. It's the purpose that reminds you *why you do what you do* on the days when the road feels steep, and it's the spark that drives you to keep creating, growing, and leading a life that reflects the very best of who you are.

Take a moment to sit with your answer. This is the heart of your *Why*. You've dug through the layers and reached the purpose that transcends goals and to-do lists. It's not just about success; it's about significance. It's about crafting a life and legacy that *matter*.

And that, my friend, is the kind of purpose that changes everything.

Now that you've completed the Five Whys, take a moment to sit with your answers.

Seriously—pause for a second. Look back over what you've written. It's fascinating, isn't it? What started as a simple, surface-level reason—perhaps something practical or straightforward—has evolved into something so much deeper and more personal. Like following a winding path through the woods, you've uncovered the core *Why* that fuels you, the purpose that sits quietly at the heart of everything you do.

This final answer? That's your compass. It's the anchor that keeps you steady when the waters get rough, the fire that keeps you moving when the days feel long, and the guiding star that helps you make decisions—big and small—with confidence.

Additional Questions for Clarity

To solidify this understanding and really let it sink in, reflect on these questions:

- **How does this purpose influence my everyday decisions?**

  Does it help you say "yes" to opportunities that align with your values and "no" to the ones that don't? Can you feel it shaping how you spend your time, build your team, or connect with clients?

- **When I face challenges, how can I remind myself of this "Why" to stay motivated?**

  Think about the tough days—because they'll come. How can you reconnect with your *Why* in those moments to push through, knowing you're working toward something that truly matters?

What actions can I take to honor this purpose in my business and personal life?

Now that you know your *Why*, what changes can you make to ensure it shows up in everything you do? Are there habits, boundaries, or new priorities that can bring you closer to living in alignment with your purpose?

By the end of this exercise, you've not just uncovered a powerful purpose—you've created clarity. This isn't just about your business goals. It's about *you*: the life you want to build, the values you hold dear, and the impact you want to make on the world. Keep this purpose close. Write it down where you can see it, let it guide you when doubt creeps in, and revisit it when you need a little extra motivation.

Wrapping Up – Additional Variations

Congratulations on completing this deep dive! Digging into the Five Whys isn't always easy—it takes honesty, reflection, and a willingness to sit with answers that sometimes surprise you. And if you've made it this far, you've already done the hard part: you've uncovered what *really* drives you.

But—and this is a friendly reminder—discovering your *Why* isn't a one-size-fits-all process. If you struggled with any part of this exercise or found your starting point didn't quite click, no worries. Jump to the final chapter, where you'll find other approaches and perspectives to help you dig deeper. Think of it as your "Purpose Toolkit"—a collection of prompts and techniques to give you new ways of looking at your values, motivations, and goals.

Here's the beauty of it: sometimes revisiting your answers from a new angle reveals insights you might have missed the first time around. Or maybe you'll stumble across a fresh perspective that makes everything click into place. The work you've done here is *foundational*, and the toolkit in the final chapter is there to help you refine and expand on it.

If, however, you're sitting there thinking, *"I've nailed it. My Why is clear, and I'm ready to roll,"* then feel free to skip ahead. You've already uncovered the kind of purpose that can fuel your journey, guide your decisions, and keep you grounded through all the twists and turns of entrepreneurship.

Either way, take a breath and congratulate yourself. Purpose-driven work isn't just about hitting goals—it's about building a life and business that reflect the very best of who you are. And that's something worth celebrating.

So here's to you, your journey, and the *Why* that makes it all worthwhile. The best is yet to come.

Chapter Five

Reflection for Self-Insight

IN THIS CHAPTER, WE'RE going to hit pause—not the frantic, "I'll deal with this later" kind of pause, but a deliberate, intentional moment to take a breath and reconnect with what truly drives you. Up until now, you've started defining your *Why*—that core purpose sitting beneath the surface of your work—and uncovering the motivations that fuel you. Now, it's time to take a step back and reflect on how well you're honoring that purpose in the day-to-day rhythm of your life and business.

Reflection is a bit like holding up a mirror to your actions and decisions, allowing you to ask the big, important questions: *Am I showing up in alignment with what matters most? Are my habits, choices, and sacrifices taking me closer to my vision, or have I drifted off course without realizing it?* These are the questions that help us recalibrate and ensure that our time, energy, and focus are being spent on what we *truly* care about—not just what's urgent or expected.

In the sections ahead, you'll find thoughtful prompts designed to guide you through this reflective process. Think of them as tools for deeper self-awareness, inviting you to explore the connection between your actions and your purpose. This isn't about critique or self-judgment; it's about curiosity and honesty. It's a chance to acknowledge where you're in sync with your *Why*—and, just as importantly, where you might need a little nudge to realign.

Why is this important? Because as entrepreneurs, it's far too easy to get swept up in the day-to-day whirlwind. The deadlines, demands, and unrelenting to-do lists have a sneaky way of clouding our sense of purpose. We find ourselves simply keeping up—doing, reacting, sprinting forward—without stopping to ask: *Am I heading in the right direction?* Self-reflection is the antidote to this kind of drift. It's what brings clarity and intention back to the journey, helping us move forward with purpose, not just momentum.

This chapter is your chance to pause, look inward, and make sure you're building the life and business you *truly* want—not just the one that's unfolding by default. Take your time with these questions. Approach them with openness, curiosity, and a willingness to listen to what surfaces. Some answers may affirm that you're exactly where you need to be, while others may nudge you toward small, meaningful shifts that bring you closer to the life you envisioned when you started this journey.

Let this be a moment of reconnection—a way to ground yourself in your *Why* and rediscover the clarity that sometimes gets buried beneath the busyness. The insights you gain here aren't just helpful; they're essential. They'll remind you of the bigger picture, the purpose guiding every decision and action, and the person you're striving to become.

So grab a notebook, find a quiet corner, and give yourself permission to slow down. Reflection is a gift, one that will guide you forward with more clarity, confidence, and intention. Let's begin.

Questions for Self-Insight

Self-reflection is like a quiet conversation with yourself—the kind where you pause, shut out the noise of the world, and get down to what *really* matters. It's a tool, yes, but also a gift. When we take the time to step back from the frantic busyness of running a business, we give ourselves the chance to reconnect—to realign our actions with the *Why* that got us started in the first place.

Here's the thing: when we're deeply connected to our *Why*, something magical happens. The chaos starts to feel less chaotic, the grind less grinding. Our day-to-day decisions begin to align naturally with our bigger goals, creating a sense of harmony between what we're doing and why we're doing it. But let's be honest—life doesn't always make that easy. It's all too common to wake up one day and realize we've been swept off course, buried under tasks, obligations, and to-do lists that feel more reactive than intentional.

And that's where these questions come in. Think of them as your compass—carefully crafted to help you pause, reflect, and come back to center. This isn't about rehashing what you already know. It's about going deeper, exploring how your *Why* can guide you more fully, not just in the big-picture vision but in the small, everyday choices that shape your journey.

- Are the decisions you're making today aligned with the purpose that brought you here?

- Are there areas where small, intentional shifts could bring you closer to a business—and a life—that feels more authentic and fulfilling?

Sometimes, it's in the subtle adjustments—reassessing priorities, releasing outdated habits, or carving out space for what truly matters—that we rediscover the clarity and energy we've been missing.

So here's what I'm asking you to do: take your time. Grab a notebook or journal, find a quiet spot (you deserve it), and let yourself settle into these questions with honesty and openness. Don't worry about coming up with perfect answers—this isn't a test. It's an opportunity to listen to yourself, to uncover insights that might surprise you, and to reaffirm the ones you already know deep down.

Some answers will be simple truths that make you nod in recognition, while others might shine a light on areas where you've drifted and didn't even realize it. Either way, this is time well spent—time that will reconnect you to the deeper motivations driving your work, the purpose that grounds you, and the vision you're building for the life and business you want.

So let's get started. This time for reflection is a gift—one that will help you refocus, realign, and move forward with greater clarity and intention.

Ready? Take a deep breath, and let's begin.

1. When did I first feel driven to start my business, and what excited me most?

Let's rewind for a moment. Take yourself back to the very beginning of this journey—back when your business was just an idea. Close your eyes and picture it. What was happening in your life at that time? What were you thinking, feeling, dreaming about?

Maybe it was the thrill of seeing a need in the world and realizing *you* could be the one to meet it. Or perhaps it was a vision of freedom, the promise of building something entirely your own. Remember how it felt when the possibilities seemed endless—when the future stretched out in front of you, untarnished by setbacks or spreadsheets.

Think about those sparks that lit you up back then. Maybe it was the creative freedom to shape something from nothing, to pour your energy into building something uniquely yours. Or perhaps it was the chance to take control of your life—your time, your decisions, your future—after years of following someone else's rules. Maybe it was more personal: the thought of making a meaningful impact on others' lives or proving to yourself (and maybe to a few skeptics) that you *could* do it.

Can you remember those late-night brainstorms where your brain refused to shut off, ideas tumbling over one another like kids racing for a playground? What about those early conversations with friends or family, where you couldn't stop talking about your vision—so much so that you probably started driving them a little nuts?

Hold onto those feelings for a minute. Let yourself feel the rush of energy, the fire that got you moving in the first place. That moment of excitement is important—it's what fueled you, what gave you the courage to step out and build something from scratch.

But here's the thing: in the day-to-day grind of running a business, it's easy to let that early passion fade into the background. The to-do lists, the challenges, the relentless march of "what's next" can drown out the very things that once made your journey feel *meaningful*. That's why this reflection matters.

Ask yourself:
- What *specifically* lit me up back then? Was it the creativity, the freedom, the challenge, or the chance to make an impact?

- Are there parts of my early excitement that I've lost touch with? Things I *used* to prioritize—like dreaming big, brainstorming new ideas, or connecting directly with clients—that I want to bring back?

- How can I reconnect with that original spark and weave it back into my work today?

Sometimes, it's in remembering those first moments—the energy, the ideas, the sense of stepping into something *big*—that we find the clarity we need to move forward. Those sparks are still there. They might be buried under layers of tasks and expectations, but they're not gone.

Let this reflection be a reminder: your journey didn't start with a spreadsheet or a sales goal. It started with a spark—one that's uniquely *yours*. By revisiting the excitement of the early days, you can refocus on what truly matters and rediscover the joy and purpose that brought you here.

And who knows? That same spark might just be the key to lighting the way forward.

2. What sacrifices have I made, and how does my "Why" justify them?

Every entrepreneur carries a ledger—one side filled with the accomplishments and milestones we proudly celebrate, and the other, a quieter tally of sacrifices made along the way. Maybe it's the family dinners missed, the vacations that never happened, or the hobbies and passions that were set aside. Perhaps it's the financial risks you've taken, the personal goals you've shelved, or the relationships that—if you're honest—felt the strain of long hours and sleepless nights.

At the time, these sacrifices often feel necessary, even inevitable. *"If I just work harder now, it will all pay off later."* That's the refrain we tell ourselves, sometimes on repeat. And while there's pride in the dedication, discipline, and grit that have gotten you this far, there's also value—real, honest value—in pausing to reflect on what these choices have *truly* cost.

Take a moment to think back.

- **What have I given up to pursue this path?** Was it time with your kids, evenings spent laughing with friends, or simple moments of rest?

- **How did those sacrifices make me feel at the time—and how do I feel about them now?** Is it pride in your resilience, regret for what you missed, or perhaps a little of both?

Allow yourself to acknowledge *all* of it. The pride and the longing. The resilience and the wistfulness. Because here's the truth: these sacrifices weren't made lightly. They were choices you made in service of something bigger—a vision, a goal, a *Why*. And that's where the power of this reflection lies: does your *Why* make these sacrifices feel worthwhile?

Ask yourself:

- **Does my purpose give meaning to the sacrifices I've made?**
  If your *Why* is clear, it can transform those sacrifices from losses into investments. When you remind yourself of *why* you've worked late nights, pushed through tough days, or poured everything you had into building your dream, it reframes the story. Those weren't just missed moments—they were choices made for something deeply meaningful to you.

But there's another layer to this reflection. What if some sacrifices *don't* feel justified by your *Why*? What if the life you're building doesn't feel as balanced or fulfilling as you hoped? That's not a failure—it's an opportunity. This is your chance to pause and realign.

- **Are there sacrifices I no longer want to make?**

- **Where can I adjust, delegate, or let go to honor the parts of my life that matter most?**

Sometimes, the reflection reveals subtle shifts that can bring your journey back into balance. Maybe it's carving out protected time for family or reconnecting with passions you've sidelined. Maybe it's delegating tasks you don't need to carry alone or creating boundaries that allow you to be *present* where it counts most.

This exercise isn't about guilt or regret; it's about clarity. Your *Why* is a guidepost—it helps you see what's worth sacrificing for and what might be better reclaimed. It reminds you that you don't have to give up everything to build something meaningful. A life that balances ambition with authenticity is not only possible; it's the life you deserve.

So, as you reflect, honor the sacrifices you've made—they've shaped who you are and brought you here. But also be brave enough to ask: *Are these the sacrifices I want to keep making?* Let your *Why* show you the way forward, giving you permission to protect what matters and release what doesn't.

At the end of the day, the goal isn't to lose yourself in the work—it's to build a life that reflects the very best of who you are and what you value most. And that, my friend, is *always* worth the effort.

3. If my "Why" could speak, what would it tell me about my current actions?

Here's where things get interesting. Picture your *Why* as a person—your wisest, most clear-headed companion. It's not the pushy, "Do more, work harder!" voice in your head. No, it's the calm, steady guide who always has your best interests at heart—someone who's deeply invested in your success *and* your well-being. Think of it like a mentor who knows exactly why you started this journey and isn't afraid to call you out when you've veered off course.

Now imagine this wise companion following you around, observing your daily choices, habits, and priorities. What would they say?

Would your *Why* nod approvingly at how you're showing up in your business and your life? Maybe it sees you carving out time for the projects that excite you, honoring your boundaries, and staying focused on the work that feels most aligned with your purpose. Perhaps it quietly applauds the moments when you choose *quality over quantity*—when you say "no" to distractions or opportunities that don't serve the bigger vision you're building.

Or... would it gently raise an eyebrow, tap you on the shoulder, and whisper a few reminders?

- Would it ask why you're working late *again*, when your purpose is rooted in freedom and time for what matters most?

- Would it question whether you've taken on too much—stretched yourself thin chasing "busy" instead of meaningful progress?

- Would it remind you that you're building a life, not just a business, and that success without fulfillment was never part of the plan?

This exercise asks for honesty—the kind of honesty that can sting a little but ultimately feels liberating. It's about stepping outside the whirlwind of to-do lists and deadlines to evaluate, with clarity and compassion, whether your current actions reflect the purpose you've worked so hard to uncover.

Ask yourself:

- **Where are my actions in harmony with my *Why*?**
  Celebrate those areas—where you're honoring your purpose through intentional choices, showing up for what matters most, and staying aligned with your vision. These moments, however small, are proof that you're on the right track.

- **Where am I out of sync?**
  Maybe your *Why* is asking you to slow down, to trust that progress doesn't come from doing *everything*, but from doing what resonates deeply. Perhaps it's nudging you to reconnect with relationships, creative passions, or parts of your life that you've sidelined for too long.

- **What habits or choices no longer serve me?**
  Your *Why* might remind you that it's okay to let go of outdated patterns—whether that's overworking, people-pleasing, or taking on pro-

jects that drain you instead of energizing you. These shifts don't have to be drastic; sometimes the smallest changes bring the greatest clarity.

By tuning in to what your *Why* would say, you're giving yourself permission to recalibrate—not out of guilt or frustration, but out of a desire to stay true to the purpose that brought you here. This process isn't about perfection. It's about progress, about making sure the life you're building feels as meaningful as the business you're running.

So ask yourself:

- If my *Why* could speak, what would it celebrate about the way I'm showing up?

- What would it lovingly encourage me to change?

Listening to this voice isn't about judgment; it's about alignment. It's an opportunity to realign your actions with your deepest motivations, to move forward with intention, and to craft a life and business that reflect the values you hold dear.

At the end of the day, your *Why* is there to guide you—not to critique you harshly, but to remind you of the bigger picture. It's a voice of clarity, one that helps you steer through the noise and get back to what *truly* matters. And when you let it lead, you're not just running a business—you're living a life that feels purposeful, aligned, and deeply your own.

Take a deep breath. Listen to that voice. Then let it guide your next step.

These questions are your guideposts—steadfast markers you can return to whenever the path ahead feels hazy or when you simply need to reconnect with what truly matters. Think of them as a personal check-in, a quiet moment to pause, breathe, and reflect. They're here to help you step back from the momentum of daily demands and ask yourself: *Am I still in harmony with the "Why" that set me on this journey?*

Because here's the truth: our lives and businesses are not static, and neither are we. As time passes, priorities shift, dreams expand, and goals evolve. Sometimes we outgrow the visions that once fueled us, or we uncover new layers of meaning we hadn't seen before. These moments of change are not detours or failures; they're invitations—gentle nudges to revisit our purpose and make sure it still aligns with the person we're becoming.

Revisiting these questions is both a grounding exercise and a celebration. It's a chance to see how far you've come—to honor the progress you've made, the lessons you've learned, and the ways you've grown. At the same time, it's a reminder of where you're headed, offering clarity and reassurance that each step forward is intentional and meaningful.

And here's the beauty of it: your *Why* doesn't need to be fixed in stone. Purpose is a living, breathing thing, growing and evolving with you as you navigate new insights, milestones, and seasons of life. Some answers may shift, and that's okay. What matters most is your willingness to show up with honesty, curiosity, and openness—allowing the truest answers to emerge, free of judgment or pressure for perfection.

So take your time. Let the reflections unfold naturally, without rushing to tie them up in a neat little bow. Authenticity is the goal here—real answers that resonate deeply and reconnect you with the reasons you care about this journey in the first place. Whether you're facing a challenge, celebrating a win, or simply feeling the need to pause and recalibrate, these questions are here to guide you back to your center.

Make this practice a regular part of your journey. Return to these reflections whenever life feels too noisy, when doubts creep in, or when you find yourself wondering whether the choices you're making are still aligned with your values and vision. By doing so, you're not just staying grounded—you're ensuring that every step forward feels true to you.

In this ever-changing landscape of entrepreneurship, these questions will be your compass. They'll remind you that success isn't just about the goals you achieve but about the person you're becoming along the way. They'll give you the confidence to navigate the twists and turns with clarity, knowing that your journey is guided by a purpose that's uniquely yours—one that supports your growth, your goals, and the legacy you're striving to build.

So keep these questions close, and revisit them often. Let them be your touchstone, your quiet reminder to keep showing up—not just for the work but for the life you're creating. And remember: the best journeys aren't defined by perfection but by intention, progress, and the unwavering pursuit of what matters most.

Prompting Self-Awareness

As entrepreneurs, our journey is rarely the neat, straight line we imagined at the start. It's more like a winding trail—full of detours, unexpected twists, and moments when we have to navigate shifting priorities or unplanned opportunities. The pressures of keeping everything moving forward can quietly pull us off course, not because we aren't focused, but because we're human. We adapt, we take on what's needed, and sometimes, without realizing it, we lose touch with the purpose that set us in motion.

This is where self-awareness becomes a powerful ally. It's the ability to pause, look honestly at where you are, and check in with the choices you're making. It's not about judgment or regret; it's about *understanding*—an honest assessment of how aligned your current actions are with the life and business you *really* want to create.

The questions in this section are your guideposts. They're here to help you step back and ask:

- *Have I drifted from my core purpose?*

- *Are the things I'm focusing on today still in harmony with the "Why" that inspired me to start this journey?*

- *And if not, what needs to change?*

Think of these reflections as an honest, compassionate check-in with yourself—a chance to recalibrate, realign, and refocus. You might find yourself looking at the sacrifices you've made and asking if they've truly served the life you envisioned. Have you taken on roles, responsibilities, or habits that don't resonate with your values, simply because they seemed necessary at the time? Have you said "yes" to opportunities that, while practical, pulled you away from the goals that mean the most?

Bringing awareness to these shifts is powerful. It allows you to see, without judgment, where subtle adjustments can bring you back to a path that feels *authentic* and fulfilling. This isn't about berating yourself for where you've drifted—it's about recognizing where you've been, honoring the progress you've made, and empowering yourself to move forward with intention.

And here's the flip side of this reflection: it's not all about what's out of sync. You'll also uncover where you're deeply aligned with your purpose. Maybe you'll notice moments where your work truly reflects your values—where you've said "no" to what doesn't serve you and prioritized what does. Recognizing those choices reinforces the things you're doing *right*—the ones that bring you joy, fulfillment, and a sense of purpose.

These questions are a mirror, showing you both the areas where you're thriving and the places where small changes could make a world of difference. With each answer, you're building a foundation of self-awareness—a clarity that empowers you to navigate the twists and turns of your journey with confidence and purpose.

Self-awareness is your compass. It doesn't demand perfection or unwavering consistency. It gives you permission to adjust, to release the things that no longer serve you, and to recommit to the actions, habits, and choices that align with your values and vision.

So embrace this reflection. Let these questions help you reconnect with the "Why" that brought you here in the first place. Allow yourself to realign where needed, and celebrate where you're already in harmony with the purpose that drives you. Because the beauty of this journey is that it's *yours*—ever-evolving, full of possibility, and guided by what truly matters to you.

And with each small shift you make, you're stepping closer to a life and business that feel deeply intentional, meaningful, and true. That's the kind of success that endures.

Chapter Six

Journaling Prompts

JOURNALING IS ONE OF those rare tools that feels both incredibly simple and profoundly transformative. It's just you, a notebook, and a pen—yet the act of writing creates space to pause, untangle your thoughts, and reconnect with what matters most. In the whirlwind of entrepreneurship, where days blur into to-do lists and decisions come at you faster than you can process, journaling becomes a quiet refuge. It's where you can slow down, take stock, and realign with the *Why* that set you on this path in the first place.

This chapter is all about making journaling accessible, intentional, and meaningful. You won't find long, complicated exercises here—just a series of thoughtful prompts designed to meet you exactly where you are. Whether you have five minutes in the morning with a cup of coffee, ten minutes before bed, or a spare moment between tasks, these prompts are your invitation to pause and reconnect.

The beauty of journaling is that it's a practice that grows with you. Some days, you might write pages, pouring out thoughts you didn't even realize were bubbling below the surface. Other days, a few sentences might be all it takes to realign your focus and spark clarity. And both are perfectly enough. The goal isn't perfection; it's *presence*. It's showing up, even briefly, to check in with yourself, your purpose, and the journey you're on.

The Challenge: 30 Days, 30 Prompts

Here's what I'm challenging you to do: dedicate just **5–10 minutes a day** for the next 30 days to journaling. Think of it as an experiment, a small investment of time to see what happens when you give yourself this space for reflection. I've provided 30 prompts to guide you through this process, each one intentionally designed to help you explore your *Why*, reflect on your decisions, and realign with the values that matter most.

If, at the end of the 30 days, you find yourself craving more (and trust me, you might), I've included **50 additional prompts** to keep the momentum going. These prompts aren't just about writing—they're about discovery. They'll help you deepen your understanding of how your purpose shapes your work, your choices, and your life. Over time, you'll start to see patterns, insights, and moments of clarity emerge.

Why Journaling Works

Here's what's magical about this practice: it strengthens your connection to your purpose, day by day. It becomes a natural filter for your decisions, helping you see where your actions align with your *Why*—and where they might need a tweak. The process isn't about adding yet another "task" to your overflowing to-do list. It's about creating a moment each day that's just for you—where you're not answering emails, solving problems, or checking boxes. You're simply reflecting, listening, and reconnecting.

Imagine what it would feel like to be so rooted in your purpose that every decision, big or small, flows from a place of clarity. That's what journaling can give you. It transforms how you show up—not just in your business but in your life.

Take the First Step

So here's my challenge to you: grab a notebook, find a quiet spot, and commit to this practice for the next 30 days. Treat it not as a chore but as a gift—a few minutes each day to refocus, realign, and reconnect with what matters most.

By the end of this month, I hope you'll not only have a stronger connection to your *Why* but also a deeper sense of purpose that shapes your days with meaning, intention, and joy. And who knows? A few scribbled sentences today might just spark the insight that transforms your tomorrow.

Let's begin.

30 Days of Journaling Prompts for Reconnecting with Your "Why"

1. Today, I'm reminded of my "Why" because...

2. One decision I made recently that aligns with my purpose is...

3. What first inspired me to start this journey, and how does it inspire me today?

4. If I could describe my "Why" in one sentence, it would be...

5. One small way I honored my "Why" today was...

6. What challenges have I faced this week, and how does my purpose help me navigate them?

7. One area of my business that reflects my core values is...

8. If my "Why" were a person, what advice would it give me right now?

9. How does my work make a difference in the lives of others?

10. One way I can realign with my purpose this week is...

11. What is one thing I'm doing now that my past self would be proud of?

12. How has my "Why" evolved over time, and what remains constant?

13. When I think of a time I felt completely aligned with my purpose, I remember...

14. What motivates me to keep going, even on tough days?

15. One habit I can develop to stay more connected to my purpose is...

16. How does my "Why" shape the way I define success?

17. If I could remove one distraction from my life, how would it bring me closer to my purpose?

18. What brings me the most joy in my work, and how does it connect to my purpose?

19. How do I want my purpose to influence the legacy I leave behind?

20. What is one fear that has kept me from fully embracing my purpose, and how can I overcome it?

21. How can I celebrate a recent accomplishment that reflects my core "Why"?

22. If my "Why" were a guiding light, what direction would it point me in right now?

23. One way I've positively impacted others through my work recently is...

24. What are three things I'm grateful for today, and how do they connect to my purpose?

25. If I could start over today, what would I do differently to stay more aligned with my "Why"?

26. How does staying true to my purpose improve my relationships with others?

27. What is one small change I can make today that would bring me closer to my "Why"?

28. When I imagine my future self, how do I see my purpose reflected in my life?

29. What is one thing I've learned about myself this month through reconnecting with my "Why"?

30. Looking back on these past 30 days, how has journaling helped me deepen my connection to my purpose?

Additional Prompts:

What does my "Why" teach me about resilience in the face of challenges?

If I described my purpose as a story, what would the main message be?

How does my "Why" influence the way I prioritize my time and energy?

What is one thing I'm doing that no longer aligns with my purpose, and how can I change it?

How does my purpose inspire others in my personal or professional life?

If I could remove one obstacle in my life, how would it help me live more in alignment with my "Why"?

What is one area of my life where I feel completely connected to my purpose?

What's one thing I've achieved that reflects my deepest values?

How do I recharge and stay motivated when I feel disconnected from my purpose?

What's a piece of advice I'd give to my younger self about staying true to my "Why"?

If I could dedicate more time to something that aligns with my purpose, what would it be?

What does success look like for me when I'm living fully aligned with my "Why"?

What's one decision I'm facing right now, and how does my purpose guide me through it?

How do I know when I'm drifting away from my "Why," and what helps me get back on track?

What role does gratitude play in helping me stay connected to my purpose?

What is one moment this week that reminded me of why I do what I do?

If I could write a letter to my "Why," what would I thank it for?

What's one lesson I've learned recently about staying true to my purpose?

How can I bring more of my personal values into my work?

What's one habit I can build to stay more aligned with my "Why"?

What inspires me about others who live in alignment with their purpose?

If I stripped away all distractions, what would remain as my core motivation?

What is one fear or doubt that keeps me from fully embracing my purpose?

What's a challenge I've faced recently, and how has my purpose helped me navigate it?

What's one way my "Why" has evolved since I started my business?

How does staying connected to my purpose influence my mental and emotional well-being?

What's one area of my life that could benefit from more alignment with my "Why"?

What's a small action I can take today to feel more connected to my purpose?

How do I want my purpose to impact the people I care about most?

What is one thing I want to teach others about the importance of purpose?

If my "Why" were a vision board, what would it look like?

What's one dream I've put on hold that aligns with my purpose?

How does my purpose help me measure progress in meaningful ways?

What's one opportunity I've embraced that reflects my "Why"?

If I weren't afraid of failure, how would I live more fully aligned with my purpose?

What's one thing I can celebrate today about how I'm living my "Why"?

How do I handle setbacks, and how does my purpose guide me through them?

What's a value I hold that's deeply connected to my purpose?

How can I simplify my life to focus more on what matters most?

What inspires me to keep showing up every day for my purpose?

What's one person who has helped me stay aligned with my "Why," and how can I thank them?

What does my ideal day look like, and how does it reflect my purpose?

What's one way I can stay more intentional in how I approach my work?

What's a new habit or routine I can develop to stay more grounded in my purpose?

What does my purpose remind me about perseverance?

What's one way my "Why" has positively shaped my business or personal life?

If I could spend more time on one thing that aligns with my purpose, what would it be?

What's one way I can bring more joy into how I approach my work?

What's a moment from the past month that reminded me of my "Why"?

How can I use what I've learned about my purpose to inspire others on their journey?

Consistency: The Key to Unlocking the Power of a Journaling

Consistency is the cornerstone of any habit that's worth its weight, and journaling is no exception. In fact, when it comes to reconnecting with your *Why* and nurturing the clarity it provides, consistency is the not-so-secret sauce. Even setting aside a few minutes each day—just you, your thoughts, and a trusty pen—can create a steady rhythm that builds a deeper, more meaningful relationship with your purpose.

Think of journaling as a conversation with yourself—an ongoing, honest dialogue where you pause, tune out the noise, and tune in to what really matters. It's a chance to *check in*: *How are you doing? Are you aligned with the vision you've set for yourself? Where are you thriving, and where do you need to shift?* These small, daily reflections act like a bridge between the grand vision in your head and the choices you make in the here and now.

Here's the beautiful thing about sticking with it: the benefits compound. At first, journaling might feel like answering prompts—helpful, but structured. But as you show up consistently, something wonderful starts to happen. Your writing evolves. You'll start noticing patterns—moments of clarity, recurring struggles, little sparks of inspiration that might have been lost in the chaos of the day. Journaling becomes less about completing an exercise and more about discovering insights that surprise you, calm you, and motivate you.

And let's be honest: life will get in the way. There will be days when journaling feels impossible. The inbox will be full, the to-do list overwhelming, and the pull to "skip today" will feel nearly irresistible. But here's the thing: *those* are the days when journaling is most powerful. Showing up when you feel overwhelmed isn't just an act of discipline—it's an act of *self-rescue*. A few quiet minutes to pause, reflect, and reconnect can be exactly what you need to steady yourself, regain perspective, and remind yourself *why you're here.*

Consistency doesn't mean perfection. It doesn't mean you need to write pages of deep, soul-searching prose every day. Some days, it's a single sentence—an honest reflection or a note to yourself about where you are and where you're going. The act of showing up, no matter how small the effort, reinforces your commitment to living and working with intention.

Think of this journaling habit as an investment. Not just in your business—though, trust me, the clarity you gain will pay dividends there—but in *you*. As an entrepreneur. As a human being. Over time, these moments of reflection will become a source of quiet strength. You'll start to approach challenges with more confidence, decisions with more clarity, and your overall journey with a sense of grounded purpose.

So keep showing up, even when it's messy, even when it's imperfect. Let the habit grow, let the insights emerge, and trust the process. Journaling isn't about writing for the sake of it; it's about building a relationship with yourself and your *Why*. And as you deepen that connection, it will guide you—day by day—toward the life and business you've always envisioned.

Pen in hand, one sentence at a time. You've got this.

Reflection and Action: Bridging Insights and Change

Reflection is powerful, no doubt about it. It's like looking into a crystal-clear pool and seeing your purpose reflected back at you. But here's the thing about insights: they're not meant to stay trapped in the journal or linger as fleeting "aha" moments. The true magic happens when those insights move you to action—when you start making small, intentional changes that bring your choices, habits, and priorities back into alignment with your *Why*.

Now, let's be clear: this doesn't mean flipping your life upside down or launching into a full-scale overhaul. That's exhausting, unsustainable, and not at all necessary. The beauty of turning reflection into action lies in simplicity. The smallest steps—when taken with intention—can create ripples that gradually transform not only your business but the way you live your life.

Each insight is a seed of potential. Maybe your journaling reveals that you've been overcommitting, saying "yes" to every opportunity that comes your way, even when they don't align with your values. Or perhaps you notice how easily meaningful priorities—like family time or creative pursuits—are being pushed to the margins, buried under the clutter of busywork. Whatever the realization, *the key is to act on it*. Even one small, deliberate step can be enough to start shifting the balance.

For instance:

- If you realize your schedule is too chaotic to focus on what matters most, your first action might be to protect a single day (or even a few hours) each week for deep, strategic work. Guard it like a bulldog guards a bone.

- If you've been sacrificing too much family time, try committing to one evening a week where you're fully present—no phones, no emails, no distractions—just time to connect with the people who mean the most.

- If you're feeling disconnected from the creative parts of your work, start small. Block out 15 minutes a day for brainstorming, writing, or dreaming up new ideas that bring you energy and joy.

It doesn't matter *how small* the action is. What matters is that it's *intentional*—a step that says, "I see what needs to change, and I'm doing something about it." These small, deliberate adjustments create momentum. One small win leads to another, and suddenly you're not just thinking about your purpose—you're living it.

Here's the beauty of marrying reflection with action: it creates a feedback loop. As you act on your insights, you start to see tangible results—more clarity, renewed energy, and a deeper sense of alignment with the life and business you're building. And those results spark even more reflection, which leads to further action, and so the cycle continues. What begins as a single small step turns into significant, lasting transformation over time.

And don't worry—taking action doesn't need to feel overwhelming. The trick is to keep it simple and consistent. One small step today. Another tomorrow. Trust that the process works, and know that every deliberate choice—no matter how minor it seems—brings you closer to the life and work that reflect what matters most to you.

In the end, *reflection and action* are two sides of the same coin. Reflection keeps you connected to your *Why*, helping you see where you're aligned and where you've drifted. Action brings that clarity to life, turning insights into momentum and dreams into reality. Together, they form a dynamic, ongoing cycle of growth—one that ensures your decisions, your business, and your life are always guided by the deeper purpose that inspired you to begin this journey in the first place.

So start small. Take that first step. And trust that those little shifts, made with intention, will carry you further than you ever thought possible.

Chapter Seven

Success Begins with Why

AND HERE WE ARE—AT the conclusion of this chapter, this book, and yet, somehow, the beginning of something much bigger. If there's one truth that has carried us through this journey, it's this: *success and fulfillment in business begin with a clear and authentic "Why."* It's not just the reason you started; it's the steady companion that keeps you grounded when the path gets bumpy, the voice of clarity in moments of doubt, and the quiet nudge that turns the everyday grind into something far more meaningful.

Think of your *Why* as your compass. When you're overwhelmed by decisions, when challenges feel insurmountable, or when you're simply unsure of what to do next, your *Why* points you back to true north. It transforms your work from a chaotic list of tasks into a deliberate, purposeful pursuit. It turns "busy" into "intentional," frustration into resilience, and goals into something that resonate with your soul.

But perhaps most importantly, a clear *Why* makes the journey itself worthwhile. Success, after all, isn't just a place you *arrive*. It's found in the small, intentional steps along the way—the challenges that teach you, the choices that align you, and the fulfillment you discover in knowing you're building something that matters.

Of course, the entrepreneurial road is rarely smooth or linear. There will be detours, uphill climbs, and moments when the path disappears entirely. It's during those times that your *Why* becomes most powerful. It's what pulls you forward when motivation wavers and helps you see that every setback, every pivot, every hard decision is still part of the larger story you're writing.

Your *Why* isn't static. It will grow and evolve alongside you, offering new insights as your life and business shift. That's the beauty of it. Your purpose isn't something you find once and lock away in a drawer. It's a living, breathing part of your journey—one you'll revisit again and again. When the road feels uncertain, go back to your *Why*. When new opportunities arise, let it help you decide which doors to walk through. And when success arrives (as it inevitably will), celebrate it as a reflection of all the ways you've stayed true to what matters most.

This chapter may feel like an ending, but really, it's an invitation—a reminder that the tools, questions, and reflections we've explored together don't expire when you close this book. They're yours to return to, to refine, and to use whenever you need to reconnect with your purpose. Because let's be honest: life will keep changing, priorities will shift, and your business will evolve. The magic is in knowing that no matter where you are or what's next, your *Why* will always be there to guide you home.

So as you step forward into the next chapter of your entrepreneurial story, carry your *Why* with you. Let it steady your steps, light your way, and inspire you to keep building—not just a successful business, but a life that feels deeply, wonderfully meaningful. The road won't always be easy, but you're ready for it.

Here's to the challenges, the victories, the growth, and the joy that lie ahead. Keep moving forward with intention, with clarity, and most of all, with purpose. You've got this.

And remember: the journey doesn't end here—it's only just beginning.

Reinforcing the Core Message

At the heart of every successful and fulfilling business lies a clear, authentic *Why*. It's more than a motivational catchphrase or a fleeting burst of inspiration—it's the bedrock upon which everything else stands. Your *Why* is the reason you take that first brave step into entrepreneurship, the force that keeps you going when the road gets rocky, and the light that shines brightest when the path ahead feels uncertain. When your *Why* is strong and deeply rooted, it becomes a compass, a steady guide that allows you to navigate the inevitable highs and lows with clarity and confidence.

Throughout this journey, we've seen just how powerful a clear *Why* can be. It serves as both anchor and inspiration, grounding you when life feels overwhelming while lifting you up with the reminder that your work has meaning. It connects even the smallest tasks to a larger purpose, turning the mundane into the meaningful. And when setbacks appear—and they always do—your *Why* provides resilience. It whispers that the effort, the late nights, the doubts are *worth it*, because what you're building matters.

But let's not stop at the hard days. Your *Why* isn't just there to steady you through storms; it's also what brings joy to the journey itself. When you're connected to your purpose, even the little victories feel momentous. A challenging project becomes a chance to stretch and grow. A milestone reached—no matter how small—feels significant because it's another step toward something meaningful. Suddenly, success is no longer just a box to tick or a finish line to cross. It's found in the journey itself—in the process of building something that reflects your values, your vision, and your dreams.

And here's the beautiful part: your *Why* will grow and evolve alongside you. You're not the same person you were when you started this journey, and you won't be the same person years from now. That's the gift of purpose: it's adaptable. It keeps pace with your life, shifting to offer guidance no matter what challenges or opportunities arise. It ensures that the success you're chasing isn't hollow or disconnected from who you are but deeply fulfilling—success that *feels* like success.

Let your *Why* be your compass. Use it to guide you through difficult decisions, to evaluate opportunities that come your way, and to remind you of what truly matters. When you feel lost, return to it like a familiar, steadying landmark. When you celebrate your victories—both big and small—let it be a reminder of the deeper meaning behind them. Your *Why* will keep you aligned, not just with the business you're building, but with the life you're creating and the legacy you'll leave behind.

So as you move forward, let your *Why* continue to light the way. Let it carry you through the challenges, amplify your triumphs, and infuse your journey with purpose. Because success isn't just about what you achieve; it's about who you become along the way. It's about creating a life and legacy that reflect the best, truest version of yourself. And that, in the end, is what makes it all worthwhile.

Chapter Eight

Living Your Why

Integrating Purpose into Every Aspect of Life & Buiness

Bringing Your Why to Life

I ONCE KNEW A man—let's call him Greg—who ran a wildly successful business but had a curious habit of frowning a lot. Not an angry scowl, mind you. More of a perplexed, furrowed-brow kind of frown, as though he'd misplaced something important but couldn't quite put his finger on what it was. One day, over coffee, I asked him what was troubling him. His answer? "I don't know why I'm doing this anymore."

Now, Greg's predicament wasn't unique. In fact, I've seen it more times than I can count. Entrepreneurs who started with big dreams—freedom, flexibility, making a difference—only to find themselves trapped in a maze of meetings, emails, and obligations that felt more like shackles than stepping stones to success. Somewhere along the way, they lost their Why, and even if they managed to rediscover it, they weren't quite sure what to do with it.

Here's the thing: finding your Why is only half the battle. The real magic happens when you take that Why—your driving purpose—and weave it into the fabric of your life. It's one thing to say, "I want my business to give me freedom." It's quite another to make decisions, set boundaries, and build routines that actually *deliver* that freedom. And let's not forget, your Why isn't just about business. It's about the life you want to live—the relationships you cherish, the impact you want to make, and the legacy you're building along the way.

Think of it like this: discovering your Why is like finding a map. You've got the directions now, but if you never actually follow them—if you just leave the map folded up on the shelf—you'll never reach your destination. Living your Why means unfolding that map and taking deliberate steps each day to align your work, your choices, and your life with the purpose that fuels you.

That's what this chapter is about. We're going to explore what it really means to *live* your Why—to make it a living, breathing part of who you are and how you show up in the world. We'll dive into how your Why can guide your decision-making, shape your daily routines, and strengthen your relationships. We'll look at how purpose can help you navigate both the exhilarating highs and the inevitable lows of entrepreneurship, keeping you grounded, focused, and resilient.

This isn't about crafting some perfect, Instagram-ready life where everything always aligns beautifully. It's about integrating your purpose into the messy, unpredictable, and wonderfully human experience of running a business and living a life. It's about showing up every day—imperfectly, perhaps, but with intention—and making choices that reflect who you are and what truly matters to you.

Because when you live your Why, something remarkable happens. Work feels less like a grind and more like a calling. Relationships deepen. Decisions become clearer. And that spark—the one that first inspired you to set out on this path—burns a little brighter, reminding you that you're not just here to build a business. You're here to build a life.

And if that's not worth showing up for every day, I don't know what is.

The Ripple Effect of Purpose

I once heard someone describe purpose as the pebble that starts a ripple in a pond. At first, you see the splash—the immediate impact in your work or business—but it doesn't take long for those ripples to reach the edges, spreading outward into every part of your life. What no one tells you, though, is that those ripples aren't always subtle little waves. They can be more like crashing surf, reshaping everything they touch in unexpected and transformative ways.

Let's be honest: most of us think of purpose in terms of work. We search for our Why because we want a business that feels meaningful, fulfilling, and aligned with who we are. But here's the surprising bit—when you connect with that Why, it doesn't just sit quietly at your desk. It follows you home. It seeps into your conversations at the dinner table, your morning routine, and even the way you interact with strangers at the grocery store. Purpose, when truly embraced, becomes a guiding principle that touches everything.

Take Sarah, a graphic designer I once worked with. She rediscovered her Why after realizing she wasn't just creating logos—she was helping people bring their dreams to life. Once that clicked, it changed more than her client list. She found herself more present with her family, more intentional about how she spent her time, and more willing to say no to things that didn't align with her values. The ripple effect wasn't just professional—it was deeply personal. Her business improved, yes, but so did her relationships, her health, and her sense of joy.

And then there's Mike, a fitness coach who started his business to help people live healthier lives. Over time, he got bogged down in the usual traps—social media metrics, revenue goals, and client retention rates. But when he reconnected with his purpose, he realized his real goal was to inspire transformation, not just track numbers. That shift changed the way he approached his work, sure, but it also changed how he showed up for his kids, his friends, and even himself. He started living the values he preached, becoming a more engaged father, a better listener, and a man who no longer worked out of obligation but out of genuine passion.

Here's the thing: when you're rooted in your Why, it doesn't stay neatly confined to business hours. It informs your choices across the board—how you manage your time, how you nurture relationships, how you contribute to your community, and even how you take care of yourself. It nudges you to be more mindful, more intentional, and more connected to the life you want to create.

Purpose-driven entrepreneurs tend to experience a curious transformation: they become better partners, parents, friends, and even neighbors. The reason? When you're clear on your Why, you're not just chasing success for success's sake. You're working toward something that feels deeply meaningful, and that meaning inevitably spills over into every part of your life.

Of course, this ripple effect isn't always dramatic. It's not about sweeping life changes that make headlines. Often, it's in the quiet moments—choosing to spend an extra hour with your kids instead of answering another email, making time for a walk instead of skipping lunch to catch up on demands, or volunteering in your community because it aligns with the values you hold dear. These small, deliberate choices accumulate, shaping a life that reflects your purpose in ways that feel genuine and fulfilling.

And that's what this section is about: recognizing that your Why isn't just a business strategy. It's a life strategy. It's about taking that spark of purpose and letting it illuminate every corner of your world.

Reflection Exercise:

Take a moment to think beyond your business. In what areas of your life do you feel a bit disconnected—where things have started to feel routine or out of sync with what you care about? Identify three non-business areas where you'd like to feel more connected to your purpose.

Maybe it's your health. Maybe it's your relationships. Maybe it's your contribution to your community or the causes that matter to you. Whatever they are, write them down. These are your ripple points—the places where your Why can create lasting change, not just in what you do, but in who you are.

Because when your Why becomes more than just a business tool, it becomes a life tool—and that's where the real transformation begins.

Practical Purpose Integration

If discovering your Why is the spark, then integrating it into your daily life is the act of keeping that fire burning. Without a consistent effort to bring purpose into the choices you make, the routines you follow, and the culture you create, your Why can fade into the background, like a motivational poster that once felt inspiring but now blends in with the wallpaper.

This section is all about making your Why a practical, living, breathing part of your daily life and business. Because let's face it, grand ideas are lovely, but if they don't show up in your actual day-to-day decisions, they remain just that—grand ideas. We're going to roll up our sleeves and figure out how to weave purpose into everything you do, so it doesn't just sit on a shelf gathering dust but becomes your compass, guiding each step you take.

Decision-Making with Purpose

Ah, decision-making. The bread and butter of entrepreneurial life. Every day presents you with a buffet of choices, from the small (should I tackle emails before or after coffee?) to the monumental (should I expand into a new market?). It's exhausting, isn't it? All those decisions stacking up like dishes in the sink.

But here's the good news: your Why can simplify this process. Think of it as a filter—a trusty sieve that sifts out the lumps, leaving behind what truly matters. When you're clear on your purpose, decisions become less about weighing endless pros and cons and more about asking one simple question: "Does this align with what I'm here to do?"

Let's say you're debating whether to take on a new client. On paper, they seem like a dream—big budget, high profile—but something feels off. Their project doesn't quite fit with your values, and you're not sure you'll feel good about the work. Without a clear purpose, you might say yes out of obligation or fear of missing out. But with your Why in hand, you can see that saying no isn't a risk—it's a choice that keeps you aligned with your core goals.

Purpose-driven decision-making doesn't just reduce overwhelm; it brings clarity. You stop chasing every opportunity and start focusing on the ones that truly matter. And let me tell you, that's a game-changer.

Quick Exercise:
The next time you're facing a decision—big or small—pause and ask yourself: "Does this move me closer to or further from my purpose?" You'll be amazed at how often the answer is clear.

Embedding Purpose into Daily Routines

Now, let's talk about routines. We all have them—whether we realize it or not. From the way you start your morning to the way you wind down at night, your days are filled with habits, both intentional and unconscious. The trick is to make sure those habits serve your purpose, not just your to-do list.

Here's a thought: what if you started each day by reconnecting with your Why? It doesn't have to be a grand ritual involving candles and chanting (unless that's your thing). It could be as simple as a morning affirmation, a quick journal entry, or a glance at a purpose statement you've pinned above your desk.

Imagine this: before diving into emails or meetings, you take a moment to remind yourself why you're doing all this in the first place. "Today, I'm working to create a life of freedom and creativity." Or, "I'm building a business that makes a positive impact." That tiny act can set the tone for your entire day.

Practical Tip:
Create a visual reminder of your Why. It could be a vision board,
a sticky note on your laptop, or a screensaver on your phone. Keep
it somewhere you'll see it often.

And don't stop there. Set aside time each week to review your goals through the lens of your purpose. Are you still aligned? Are you making progress toward what truly matters? A quick check-in can prevent you from veering off course.

Creating a Purpose-Driven Culture

If you're leading a team—whether it's a full staff or a handful of contractors—your purpose doesn't just live inside your head. It needs to be shared. Infused into the culture of your business. Because when everyone is aligned with the Why, magic happens.

Think about the businesses you admire. Chances are, they're not just selling products or services; they're selling a story, a mission, a reason for being. Customers feel it. Employees feel it. There's a sense of connection that goes beyond transactions. That's the power of a purpose-driven culture.

Start by sharing your Why with your team. Not as a corporate memo, but as a conversation. Let them know what drives you and invite them to share their own purpose. When people understand the bigger picture, they're more engaged, more motivated, and more connected to the work they do.

Example:
I once worked with a business owner who made it a point to start every team meeting with a purpose check-in. Not a long, drawn-out session—just a quick reminder of why they were there. "Our mission is to help small businesses thrive." It took less than a minute, but it set the tone for everything that followed.

And don't forget your customers. Share your Why in your marketing, your conversations, and your customer interactions. People want to feel connected to something bigger. Give them that connection, and you'll build loyalty that goes beyond the product or service you offer.

Bringing It All Together

Purpose isn't just a nice idea to ponder over coffee. It's a practical tool that can shape every part of your life and business. When you use your Why as a filter for decisions, embed it into your routines, and share it with those around you, you're not just talking about purpose—you're living it.

The best part? Purpose-driven entrepreneurs don't just succeed in business. They build lives that feel meaningful, fulfilling, and deeply connected to what matters most. And that, my friend, is the real definition of success.

Evolving with Your Why

Ah, evolution. It's the reason your smartphone now has more computing power than the spacecraft that landed on the moon, and why your taste in music has (hopefully) progressed beyond whatever questionable choices you made as a teenager. And just like your music playlist and technology, your Why isn't meant to stay frozen in time. It grows, shifts, and adapts, reflecting where you are in life and where you want to go.

In this section, we'll dive into how your purpose can evolve, how to recognize when you've drifted from it, and how to weave it into your long-term goals to keep your journey meaningful and fulfilling.

Purpose Isn't Static

When you first discovered your Why, it probably felt like the golden key to everything—clear, shiny, and unshakeable. But life, as it tends to do, has a way of complicating things. Businesses grow, personal priorities shift, and before you know it, the Why that once fit like a glove starts feeling a bit snug. And that's okay. Purpose isn't meant to be static.

Think of your Why as a compass, not a destination. The compass always points to true north, but the path you take to get there can change with the terrain. Maybe your original Why was about achieving financial independence. But as your business took off, you realized that what truly lights you up is creating opportunities for others. That's an evolution, not a betrayal of your original purpose.

Example:

Take Rachel, a client of mine who launched a business to achieve financial freedom. In the early days, her Why was crystal clear—build something that allowed her to escape the 9-to-5 grind. But as her business grew, she found herself more passionate about mentoring others. Her purpose shifted from personal freedom to empowering her team and clients. That shift brought new energy and clarity to her work.

Adapting your Why isn't a sign that you've lost your way. It's proof that you're growing, learning, and evolving. And that's what keeps life interesting, isn't it?

Recognizing Signs of Drift

Of course, sometimes we don't realize we've drifted until we're halfway to somewhere we didn't intend to go—like ending up at a furniture store on a Saturday when all you wanted was a quiet coffee. The same thing can happen with your Why. You think you're moving forward, but one day you look around and wonder, "How did I end up here?"

There are signs that you've lost alignment with your purpose, but they're often subtle at first:

- **Burnout**: Work feels more exhausting than energizing.

- **Lack of Motivation**: The tasks you once enjoyed now feel like a chore.

- **Frustration**: You find yourself snapping at small things or feeling perpetually stuck.

When these feelings creep in, it's time to pause. And I mean really pause—none of that "I'll reflect while I multitask" nonsense. Give yourself permission to step back and ask, "Am I still on the path I want to be on?"

And here's the kicker: be kind to yourself in this process. Drift happens to all of us. It's not a failure; it's an opportunity to re-center and get back to what matters.

Reflection Exercise:

Set aside time to journal about your current feelings toward your work. Are you excited, content, or drained? Write down three things that feel aligned with your Why and three that don't. This simple exercise can help you pinpoint where adjustments are needed.

Purpose in Milestones

Now, let's talk about milestones. Entrepreneurs love them. We set goals, chase them with reckless abandon, and then... what? We tick the box and immediately set another goal. The celebration lasts about as long as a cup of coffee before we're off to the next thing.

But what if your milestones weren't just about achievement? What if they were about alignment?

Anchoring your Why into your milestones changes the entire game. Instead of chasing arbitrary targets, you're celebrating progress toward what truly matters to you.

Example:

Imagine two entrepreneurs. One hits a revenue target and celebrates with a generic "We did it!" post on social media. The other hits the same target but reflects on how that milestone brings them closer to their purpose—whether it's creating more flexibility, supporting a cause they care about, or providing for their family. Which one do you think feels more fulfilled?

When your milestones are tied to your purpose, each achievement feels richer, more meaningful. And you're less likely to fall into the trap of chasing success for success's sake.

Quick Tip:
When setting goals, ask yourself, "How does this milestone connect to my Why?" If it doesn't, it might be time to reconsider whether it's worth pursuing.

Bringing It All Together

Purpose isn't a fixed point on a map; it's a living, evolving part of who you are. As you grow, so will your Why. Recognizing and embracing that evolution is what keeps your journey fresh, exciting, and deeply meaningful.

And when you anchor your milestones to that purpose, something magical happens. Success stops feeling like a checklist and starts feeling like a story—a story that reflects your values, your growth, and the legacy you're building.

Because, in the end, it's not just about where you're going. It's about why you're going there. And when your Why evolves alongside you, the journey becomes infinitely more rewarding.

Purpose Check-Ins

Ah, the check-in—a concept most of us associate with airport counters, social media updates, or mildly awkward work meetings. But when it comes to your Why, a check-in isn't just a courtesy. It's a lifeline. It's a way to make sure that your purpose is still, well, purposeful. Because here's the thing: life moves fast, businesses evolve, and what once lit you up might need a little dusting off from time to time.

In this section, we're going to explore the art of the **Purpose Check-In**—a simple yet profound habit that keeps your Why relevant, alive, and deeply connected to your goals. Think of it as a quarterly tune-up for your soul.

The Importance of Reflection

Let's be honest—most of us don't pause nearly as often as we should. We're too busy tackling today's to-do list while mentally drafting tomorrow's. But when you don't take the time to reflect, your Why can start to feel more like an old keepsake collecting dust in the attic rather than the guiding compass it's meant to be.

Here's the truth: your Why isn't a one-and-done discovery. It's not something you figure out once and then put on a shelf. It needs care, attention, and, yes, the occasional adjustment. That's where regular check-ins come in.

Reflection helps you make sure that the path you're on still aligns with the person you've become and the goals you're pursuing. It's easy to get caught up in the hustle, chasing goals that sounded good a year ago but no longer resonate. A purpose check-in gives you the chance to pause and ask:

- **Does my Why still align with my current goals?**

- **Am I making choices that reflect my core values?**

- **What has changed since my last check-in, and how do I feel about those changes?**

Without reflection, it's all too easy to wake up one day and realize you've built a life or business that looks good on paper but feels hollow inside. Check-ins help you avoid that pitfall. They keep you grounded and ensure that your actions are still aligned with your heart.

Introducing Purpose Audits

Now, let's add a bit of structure to this. Enter the **Purpose Audit**—a fancy name for what is essentially a regular sit-down with yourself to take stock of where you're at, where you're going, and, most importantly, why you're doing it.

Here's how it works:

Quarterly Purpose Check-In
Think of this as a seasonal recalibration. Every three months, set aside time to reflect on your purpose and how it's showing up in your business and life. Ask yourself:

- What have I accomplished this quarter that aligns with my Why?

- Where have I drifted, and why?

- What adjustments can I make to bring myself back into alignment?

The quarterly check-in doesn't need to be a marathon journaling session (though, by all means, grab your notebook if that's your style). It can be a simple, intentional conversation with yourself—over coffee, on a walk, or wherever you do your best thinking. The goal is to catch any signs of drift before they become full-on detours.

Annual Purpose Audit
Ah, the big one. Once a year, go deeper. This is your chance to do a comprehensive review of your Why and how it's evolved over the past year. Reflect on:

- How has my Why changed?

- What goals still feel relevant, and which ones need updating?

- Am I still building a life and business that align with my values?

The annual audit is also a great time to celebrate your progress. Too often, we focus on what's next without acknowledging how far we've come. Taking stock of your wins—both big and small—reinforces your connection to your purpose and keeps you motivated for the year ahead.

What to Look for in a Purpose Check-In

When you're doing these check-ins, keep an eye out for key signs that you're drifting from your Why:

- You feel constantly exhausted, even when things are going well.

- Your goals feel more like obligations than inspirations.

- You're saying "yes" to things that don't align with your values.

And here's a gentle reminder: it's perfectly okay if your Why evolves. In fact, it should. Your life changes, your priorities shift, and your purpose can—and will—adapt to reflect those changes. The key is to stay aware of those shifts so you can make intentional adjustments rather than getting swept along by the current.

Bringing It All Together

Purpose isn't a set-it-and-forget-it kind of thing. It's a living, breathing part of who you are, and it deserves your attention. Regular check-ins—whether quarterly, annually, or whenever you feel the need—ensure that you're staying true to what matters most.

So grab your calendar, block out some time, and commit to making Purpose Check-Ins a regular part of your routine. Because when you stay connected to your Why, you're not just running a business. You're building a life that feels right—every step of the way.

Questions for a Purpose Check-In:

- What is my *Why* today, and does it still feel true?

- How have my actions over the past few months aligned with my purpose?

- What adjustments can I make to bring my work and life closer to my *Why*?

Living with Intention

Let's talk about maps for a moment. If you've ever gone on a road trip—or, more accurately, if you've ever found yourself hopelessly lost on a road trip—you'll know that a good map is invaluable. But here's the thing: maps aren't just about getting you to a single destination. They help you navigate twists and turns, unexpected detours, and the occasional "Why is there a goat in the road?" moment. And that's precisely what living with intention is all about. Your Why is not a pin on a map; it's the map itself, guiding you through the unpredictable terrain of life and business.

Purpose as a Way of Moving Through the World

Too often, we treat purpose as if it's something we'll discover at the end of a long journey. It's out there, somewhere on the horizon, waiting to reveal itself when we've achieved enough, worked hard enough, or reached some elusive milestone of success. But here's the truth: your Why isn't a destination you'll one day arrive at with a victorious shout and a celebratory confetti cannon. It's the way you move through the world, the lens through which you view your choices, and the compass that keeps you aligned with what matters most.

When you live with intention, every action—big or small—has meaning. You're no longer just reacting to what life throws at you; you're making deliberate choices that reflect your values and your vision. Living your Why isn't about perfection. It's not about never making mistakes or always knowing the right answer. It's about showing up, every day, with a clear sense of who you are and what you're working toward.

And here's the best part: living with intention doesn't just transform your business. It transforms your entire life.

A Lifelong Companion

Think of your Why as that trusted friend who always gives it to you straight. The one who reminds you to stay true to yourself, even when the world tries to pull you in a hundred different directions. Your Why isn't a fleeting spark of motivation; it's a lifelong companion, walking beside you through every success, setback, and surprising plot twist.

When you're aligned with your Why, you're more resilient in the face of challenges. You make decisions with clarity, not because you've weighed every possible pro and con, but because you know what feels right. You find fulfillment not in some distant finish line, but in the everyday moments—the small wins, the meaningful connections, the work that lights you up.

And yes, life will change. Your goals will evolve. The business you're running today might look completely different in five years. But your Why? That core purpose? It will adapt with you, growing stronger with each experience, each lesson, and each step forward. The more you live with intention, the more your Why becomes ingrained in every part of who you are.

Transforming Your Life and the Lives You Touch

Here's the beautiful thing about living your Why: it doesn't just impact you. It ripples outward, touching everyone you interact with. Your clients feel it. Your team feels it. Your family and friends feel it. Purpose is contagious in the best possible way. When you're clear on your Why and living with intention, you inspire others to do the same.

You create a business that doesn't just meet targets, but makes a meaningful impact. You cultivate relationships that aren't just transactional, but deeply connected. And you build a life that isn't just busy or productive, but fulfilling—rich with experiences, values, and moments that truly matter.

So as we wrap up this journey together, let me leave you with this:

Your Why isn't something you discover once and then set aside like a dusty trophy on a shelf. It's a living, breathing part of who you are. It grows with you, evolves with you, and strengthens you. It's the quiet voice that reminds you why you started, the steady compass that keeps you on course, and the spark that lights your way through the darkest of days.

Live with intention. Lead with purpose. And remember that every step you take—when guided by your Why—is a step toward a life that's not just successful, but deeply meaningful.

And if ever you find yourself wondering, "Am I on the right path?" just pause, take a breath, and listen to that steady voice within. Your Why is always there, waiting to guide you home.

Exercise: Purpose in Practice Plan – Living Your Why in Real Life

Purpose is a lovely idea, isn't it? It makes us feel grounded, inspired, and ready to take on the world. But here's the thing—purpose only works if we *live* it. It's not meant to sit prettily on a vision board, gathering dust like an old souvenir. It's meant to be woven into the fabric of your daily life, guiding your actions, decisions, and even your outlook on those "did-I-really-sign-up-for-this?" days.

So, let's put your Why to work with a **Purpose in Practice Plan**—a simple, actionable guide to help you live your purpose in a meaningful way over the coming weeks.

Step 1: Choose Your Focus Area

Think about an area of your life where you've been feeling disconnected or stuck. This could be your business, personal relationships, health, or even your community involvement.

Ask yourself: *Where would living my Why make the biggest impact right now?* For example:

- If your business has felt like an endless grind, maybe you want to focus on purpose-driven decision-making.

- If your personal relationships have taken a backseat, perhaps reconnecting with your Why could help you show up more intentionally for the people who matter.

- If your health has been neglected in favor of long work hours, aligning your actions with your Why could remind you that taking care of yourself isn't optional—it's essential.

Write it down: **My focus area is:** _____

Step 2: Set a Purpose-Driven Goal

Now that you've identified where you want to focus, let's set a goal that connects to your Why. Remember, this goal should reflect *why you started in the first place*—whether it's freedom, creativity, making an impact, or building a legacy.

For example:

- **Business goal:** "I want to create a work schedule that allows me to prioritize creative projects that reignite my passion."

- **Personal relationship goal:** "I want to be more present and intentional with my family, reducing distractions during our time together."

- **Health goal:** "I want to incorporate small, sustainable habits that support my long-term well-being."

Write   it   down: **My   purpose-driven   goal   is:**

_____

Step 3: Outline Three Small, Aligned Actions

Big goals are wonderful, but let's be honest—they can also feel overwhelming. The key to making progress is to break your goal into small, manageable actions that align with your Why.

For example:

- **Business:**

a. Block out one hour a week for creative work.

b. Say "no" to one low-priority project this month.

c. End work at a set time each day to avoid burnout.

- **Personal Relationships:**

    a. Put away your phone during meals.

    b. Schedule a family activity that you've been putting off.

    c. Write a note or send a message of appreciation to someone you care about.

- **Health:**

    a. Take a 10-minute walk each day.

    b. Prep healthy meals once a week to reduce stress during busy days.

    c. Set a bedtime alarm to remind yourself to prioritize sleep.

Write it down: **Three small actions I'll take:**

Step 4: Commit to a Check-In in 30 Days

Here's where the magic happens—reflection.

Commit to revisiting your Purpose in Practice Plan in 30 days. Take stock of what worked, what didn't, and how you felt throughout the process. Did you feel more connected to your Why? Did it shift the way you approached your work, relationships, or self-care? And most importantly—what adjustments do you want to make for the next month?

Write it down: **I will check in on my plan on:**

A Few Gentle Reminders

- **Progress beats perfection.** Even one small action in alignment with your Why is better than staying stuck in the hamster wheel.

- **Be kind to yourself.** This is a journey, not a sprint. Some days you'll feel on top of the world, and other days you'll want to stay under the covers. Both are okay.

- **Keep your Why visible.** Whether it's a sticky note on your desk, a reminder on your phone, or a little mantra you say to yourself each morning—keep your Why front and center. It'll help you stay grounded when life gets chaotic.

Final Thought: Your Why, in Action

Living your Why isn't a one-and-done task. It's a daily practice—a way of moving through the world with intention, clarity, and purpose. And this plan? It's just the beginning.

Take these small steps, one by one, and watch how your world shifts. The impact won't just be in your business. It'll ripple out into every part of your life, bringing with it a sense of fulfillment that's rooted in what truly matters to you.

Bonus: A Variation on the Exercise

"The Five Whys"

Introduction to Variations of "Why Did I Start My Business?

ANSWERING THE QUESTION *"WHY did I start my business?"* can uncover a vast range of motivations. Some are practical—a desire for financial independence, freedom, or growth. Others are deeply personal—rooted in values, passions, or a longing to make a difference. No matter where you begin, each answer holds the potential to reveal something important about your unique purpose, helping you uncover what truly matters most.

It's surprisingly easy to find yourself on a path that doesn't feel like your own. Well-meaning advice, external expectations, or even comparisons to other entrepreneurs can lead you away from your original intentions. My goal here isn't to point you toward a "right" answer—because there isn't one. Instead, I want to guide you in rediscovering the answer that feels most *authentic* to you.

To inspire your thinking, here are a few common starting points that many entrepreneurs identify when they reflect on their beginnings:

- **I wanted to create something of my own.**

- **I wanted to challenge myself and grow personally.**

- **I saw a need in the market that I felt passionate about solving.**

- **I wanted financial independence.**

- **I wanted to pursue a career that aligned with my values.**

Perhaps one of these resonates with you immediately. Maybe it sparks a memory of what first lit that fire within you. Or it could remind you of a unique, deeply personal reason for starting this journey that isn't listed here—one that's entirely your own.

Each of these starting points can act as a springboard for deeper exploration. What you begin with is rarely where you'll finish. Your answer might start simple—"I wanted to be my own boss"—but when you take the time to ask *why* that mattered, you begin to uncover layers of meaning, values, and dreams that lie beneath the surface.

Let me illustrate with a quick example:

Starting Point: I wanted financial independence.

Why is that important? It would allow me to take care of my family without stress.

Why does that matter? Because I grew up watching my parents struggle financially, and I wanted to break that cycle for my children.

What does that mean to me now? It means building a business that creates stability, security, and opportunities for my family, while still allowing me to be present with them.

This example shows how even a straightforward answer can lead you to something deeply personal and powerful. It's this kind of exploration that turns surface-level motivations into a *Why* that keeps you grounded, inspired, and aligned with what truly matters.

Feel free to use this exercise as a prompt for your own reflection. Begin with the reason that first comes to mind—don't overthink it—and let yourself explore. If you need more structure, revisit Chapter 4 for a detailed walk-through of the process.

Most importantly, take your time. Your purpose is unique to you, and finding it is about staying true to the motivations that resonate most with your life, your values, and your dreams. Every moment spent reflecting brings you one step closer to uncovering the foundation that gives your work its deepest meaning.

This isn't just about where you started—it's about reconnecting to the purpose that will guide you forward. Let's get started.

Variation on the Theme

Step 1: Initial Reason – Why Did I Start My Business?

Begin by writing down your *first instinctive answer* to why you started your business. Think back to those early days—before the plans, the strategies, or the to-do lists took over. What was the initial spark that set you on this path? Don't overthink it, and don't worry if the answer feels simple or obvious. It doesn't need to be profound or poetic—it just needs to be *yours*.

This first response is your starting point. It's the surface-level motivation that launched your journey, and from here, we'll dig deeper to uncover the deeper layers of your *Why*.

Example: *I wanted to help people.*

Write it down—clear and simple. Honor this first reason, because it's what got you moving in the first place. This is where your exploration begins.

Step 2: First "Why?" – Why Is Helping People Important to Me?

Now that you've identified your starting point, it's time to take it one step further. Ask yourself: *Why does this matter to me?* Why is helping others—or whatever your initial reason was—important on a deeper level?

Take a moment to consider what it brings to your life. Does it fulfill you emotionally, giving you a sense of meaning and connection? Does it align with your values, the kind of person you want to be, or the impact you want to leave on the world? Maybe it reflects experiences you've had, lessons you've learned, or people who've inspired you.

Write your answer with honesty and openness. Let yourself explore the emotional, practical, or even spiritual reasons behind why this matters.

Example: *Helping people gives me a sense of purpose and makes me feel like I'm making a positive impact.*

With this step, you're beginning to uncover what lies beneath your initial reason—connecting your motivation to something that resonates more deeply with who you are and what you value.

Step 3: Second "Why?" – Why Does Making a Positive Impact Give Me a Sense of Purpose?

Here's where we dig a little deeper. Take your previous answer and ask yourself: *Why does this matter to me?* Why does making a positive impact feel so significant?

Reflect on what it means for you personally. Does it help you feel connected to others, as though you're part of something bigger than yourself? Does it align with values you hold close—like kindness, contribution, or leaving the world a little better than you found it? Or maybe it's tied to a deeper sense of fulfillment—something that brings you peace, meaning, and pride in how you're showing up in life.

Consider how making a positive impact shapes your identity, your role in the world, and the legacy you want to leave behind. This step isn't about perfection—it's about discovering what truly resonates within you.

Example: *Making a positive impact helps me feel connected to others and gives my life meaning.*

By asking this second *Why*, you're uncovering not just what you do, but the personal significance it holds—moving another step closer to the heart of your deeper purpose.

Step 4: Third "Why?" – Why Is Feeling Connected to Others and Living a Life of Meaning Important to Me?

At this stage, you're getting closer to the core values that drive your motivation. Take a moment to reflect on *why* these feelings of connection and meaning matter so deeply to you.

Ask yourself:

- What does being connected to others bring to my life?

- Why does living a meaningful life feel so vital for my sense of fulfillment and well-being?

- Does it help me feel grounded, purposeful, or at peace?

- Is it about belonging, leaving a legacy, or contributing to something greater than myself?

Let your answer explore how these values shape who you are and how you want to experience the world. This is where your *Why* starts to feel bigger, connecting you to a broader sense of purpose and identity.

Example: *Feeling connected to others and having a meaningful life helps me feel that I'm part of something bigger than myself.*

With this reflection, you're revealing the deeper threads of your motivation—values like connection, contribution, or legacy. These are the forces that give your work and life a greater sense of meaning and direction.

Step 5: Fourth "Why?" – Why Do I Want to Feel Like I'm Part of Something Bigger Than Myself?

Now, you're digging into the heart of your deeper motivations. Ask yourself: *Why is this feeling of being part of something greater so important to me?* Why does it resonate with who I am, the goals I hold, or the legacy I want to leave behind?

Consider:

- Does it give you a sense of purpose beyond the day-to-day tasks?

- Does it remind you that your actions, however small, have meaning and impact?

- Does it align with your identity as someone who wants to contribute, make a difference, or leave the world better than you found it?

This reflection brings you closer to your "Why" by uncovering the values, hopes, and bigger-picture desires that drive you forward.

Example: *Feeling part of something bigger reminds me that my actions matter and that I can contribute to positive change in the world.*

At this step, you're discovering that your purpose isn't just about business—it's tied to a broader impact. You're uncovering the deeper significance behind your actions and connecting your work to something truly meaningful and lasting.

Step 6: Fifth "Why?" – Why Does Knowing My Actions Matter and Contribute to Positive Change Bring Me Fulfillment?

You've reached the final layer—the heart of what truly drives you. Take a moment to reflect deeply on why knowing your actions make a difference and contribute to positive change holds such profound meaning for you.

Ask yourself:

- How does this connect to who I am at my core?

- Why does leaving the world better than I found it matter to me?

- How does this desire align with the life I want to lead or the legacy I want to leave behind?

This is where your purpose reveals itself in its purest form. It's no longer about goals, milestones, or tasks. It's about the *impact* you hope to make and the kind of person you want to be remembered as.

Example: *Knowing my actions matter and contribute to positive change allows me to leave the world better than I found it, creating a lasting legacy of kindness and compassion.*

Here, you've uncovered the deep purpose behind your journey. It's not just about helping people or building a business—it's about creating a life that reflects your values, leaves a meaningful impact, and resonates with the person you strive to be. This is your "Why"—the foundation that fuels everything you do and the compass that will guide you forward.

Reflection

Through this exercise, you've unearthed a purpose that reaches far beyond the surface—beyond simply "helping people" or running a successful business. At the very core, you're driven by a profound desire to connect meaningfully with others, leave a positive impact, and contribute to a kinder, more compassionate world. This isn't just a mission; it's a guiding force that weaves its way through every part of your life, reminding you that your actions matter and that you're building something far greater than a business. You're building a legacy rooted in care, connection, and positive change.

With this newfound clarity, pause and ask yourself how this purpose can become the foundation for your next steps:

- **How can it guide your business decisions?** Will it inspire you to take on only the projects that align with this deeper vision, ensuring every "yes" reflects the values you hold dear?

- **How will it shape your relationships?** Let this purpose deepen how you connect with your team, your clients, your family—bringing more authenticity and care into every interaction.

- **How will it strengthen you during challenges?** Let it remind you that setbacks are temporary, but a life lived with intention and integrity leaves an impact that lasts.

This purpose is your compass. It gives every task, every challenge, and every win deeper meaning. When the path ahead feels uncertain or the noise of the day-to-day pulls you off track, come back to this core. It's your anchor, your guiding light, and your reminder of what truly matters most.

With this clarity, you're not just running a business—you're building a life, a legacy, and a contribution to the world that reflects the very best of who you are. Let it guide you forward with confidence, focus, and a sense of fulfillment that grows with every step.

About the Author

MEET ROGER BEST

Roger Best is a seasoned entrepreneur who's navigated the wild ride of building multiple successful businesses. With years of battle scars and triumphs, he knows firsthand the relentless grind of entrepreneurship—those long hours, high-stakes decisions, and the relentless chase for success that can sometimes steal the joy out of life.

But Roger isn't just a survivor; he's a thriver. After his own transformation from a business owner burning the candle at both ends to a man who's mastered the balance of work and play, he's on a mission to help others break free from the chains of the endless hustle. In this book, he lays out practical, no-nonsense strategies to reclaim your time, achieve financial freedom, and craft a life packed with purpose, adventure, and a healthy dose of leisure.

When Roger's not in the trenches with one of his ventures, writing, or mentoring fellow entrepreneurs, you'll find him living life on his terms—spending quality time with family and friends, exploring new terrain, or just kicking back and enjoying the satisfaction that comes from running a successful business that doesn't dominate every moment.

Roger's been married to his soulmate for just over 45 years, a proud dad to two grown kids, and a devoted grandfather to two little princesses. In 2021, he and his wife decided to turn their island dream into reality, moving to Puerto Rico, where they now run their businesses while soaking up the hammock life.

Roger's mission is straightforward: to inspire and empower entrepreneurs to build thriving businesses without sacrificing their happiness, health, or freedom.

Also by Roger Best

If you enjoyed this book, you might be interested in reading other books written by Roger Best:

Getting Your Day Back Series

From Hamster Wheel to Hammock: A Guide to Taking Your Day Back – Book 1

Are you trapped in the endless grind, feeling overworked and disconnected from the life you've always dreamed of? Imagine lounging on a hammock, sipping mojitos, and enjoying the true essence of life. "From Hamster Wheel to Hammock: A Guide to Taking Back Your Day" is your roadmap to living that dream without sacrificing your business.

Packed with reflective exercises, mindset shifts, and real-life examples, this book empowers you to redefine success and reclaim your ideal lifestyle. Are you ready to step off the hamster wheel and start living? Take the first step towards the life you deserve. Reclaim your time, redefine your success, and embrace a life of purpose and joy.

Transform your life today with "From Hamster Wheel to Hammock." Your ideal lifestyle awaits.

Personal Growth for Entrepreneurs: Your Time, Your Way – Book 2

In *Personal Growth for Entrepreneurs: Your Time, Your Way*, you'll discover the power of reclaiming control over your time and making intentional choices that align with your personal and professional goals. This book is designed for entrepreneurs who are tired of the relentless hustle, looking to step off the hamster wheel, and ready to create a more balanced, fulfilling life.

Through practical strategies and actionable advice, you'll learn how to break free from the cycles of busyness, manage your time more effectively, and refocus on what truly matters—your growth, your goals, and your well-being. You'll explore how to shift your mindset, set boundaries, simplify your daily routines, and make space for the things that truly nourish you.

This book goes beyond just productivity hacks. It's about empowering you to live and work with intention, rediscover your passions, and create a life that feels deeply fulfilling—on your terms, your way.

If you're ready to take back control of your time and thrive both personally and professionally, *Personal Growth for Entrepreneurs* is your guide to making that a reality.

www.ingramcontent.com/pod-product-compliance
Lightning Source LLC
Chambersburg PA
CBHW071527120626

46550CB00006B/2382